PENGUIN BOOKS

Chinese

Chinese

Jacki Passmore

Contents

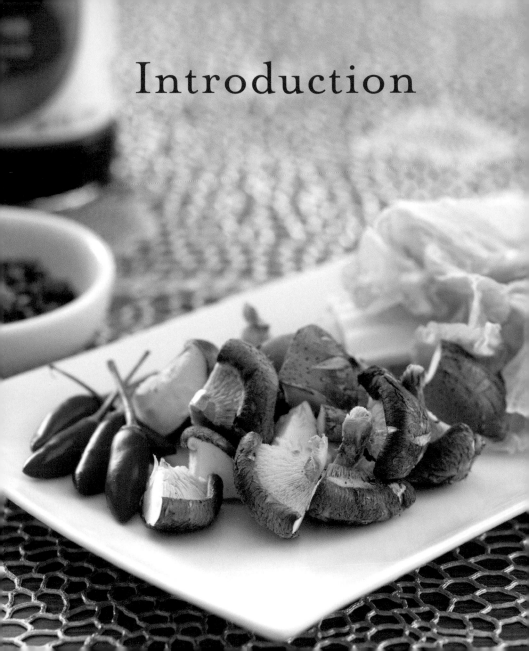

Introduction

If you are new to Chinese cooking, take a look through these delicious recipes—you'll find that most home-style Chinese cooking is quick and easy, and requires little in the way of special equipment. Add a wok, a steamer and a cleaver to your kitchen, and you're ready to go.

Fresh Chinese vegetables are now easy to find, as are all of the basic sauces, noodles and condiments. If you can't find a particular ingredient at your local supermarket, there's bound to be an Asian food store nearby—a look through their jam-packed shelves is an adventure in itself!

Chinese Basics

There's no single word to describe Chinese cuisine, except perhaps 'amazing'. Like China itself—with its teeming population, spectacular scenery and eventful history—no other cuisine offers so much to entice us, so much to enjoy and experience.

The cuisine can be divided into a few major regional cooking styles—although this is a somewhat simplistic approach, it allows us to gain some understanding of the wide-ranging tastes and different cooking methods preferred across the vast country.

In the south, where rice paddies are carved into every hillside, subtle flavors and clear sauces characterize the cuisine. Pork is roasted to crackling perfection for celebratory feasts and fresh vegetables are cooked in tiered steamers or tossed in sizzling woks.

Eastern coastal cuisine works magic with seafood, and the fishermen of the region sail their lumbering wooden junks far into the surrounding seas to catch the freshest fish and exotic marine life.

The regional cuisine of the central Sichuan and Hunan provinces is noted for its salty bean sauces, chili peppers and fragrant, mouth-numbing local pepper. The food of the far west has a distinctly Muslim appeal with its spicy lamb dishes and skewered meats.

In the north, wheat outpaces rice in popularity—it is made into hand-stretched noodles, and baked, grilled or steamed into soft-textured breads, buns and dumplings. Tender pancakes wrap slivers of succulent roast duck. Sauces are redolent of rice wine, garlic and soy.

The Chinese Table

While a banquet meal at a Chinese restaurant comprises many courses—beginning with tasty little appetizers, followed by several main dishes served banquet style, and finishing with platters of fresh fruit—family meals are usually simple affairs, consisting of one or two dishes served with rice, or perhaps just a single heaped platter of noodles.

When cooking for friends, you may prefer to divide a meal into distinct courses, with a starter or soup to begin, a single main dish accompanied by rice or noodles and a vegetable dish, followed by a sweet or dessert to finish. Cooking at the table, such as for Mongolian steamboat or Sichuan hotpot, is an enjoyable way to entertain, as everyone gets into the action. Once you've gained confidence, you might want to try making a full dim-sum meal; serving baskets of dumplings, tender meats and crunchy fried snacks.

Hot green or black tea, served in small cups from a teapot, is the standard beverage offered with all meals in China. If you prefer wine, choose a crisp, light white for stir-fries and seafood, and a pinot noir or other light red for duck, beef or lamb dishes.

To capture the true style of the Chinese table, you can purchase authentic bowls, chopsticks and other tableware from Chinese stores.

The Chinese Kitchen

You'll find that most home-style Chinese cooking is quick and easy, and requires little in the way of special equipment. Add a wok, flat spatula, and cleaver to your kitchen equipment and you're ready to go. (While a Chinese cleaver seems large and heavy at first, you'll find with practice that it is a most practical and versatile tool for just about every cutting and slicing chore you'll face.) Although not essential, a pair of steamer tongs for lifting dishes from the steamer can be helpful.

Wok cooking is best done over high heat, and many domestic gas cookers are now fitted with a wok ring. A portable gas wok cooker or a wok ring attached to your barbecue is an excellent alternative if you'd rather keep the smoke and splashes out of the kitchen.

Steaming is an important Chinese cooking method. You can purchase a tiered steamer or steamer baskets from a

Chinese store, or use a standard steamer insert in a sauce-pan — or do as many Chinese cooks do and use the wok and its domed lid with a steamer rack or a pair of wooden chopsticks for supporting the plate or bowl inside.

For slow cooking, braising and poaching, a heavy-based saucepan or a clay or terracotta pot will be perfect. The wok is an excellent vessel for deep-frying, while any good fry pan works well for shallow-frying.

Cooking Techniques

STIR-FRYING

Stir-frying is done in a wok over very high heat. Heat the wok first, then add the oil and swirl the wok to coat the inside cooking surface. Heat until the oil just begins to smoke before adding ingredients. Cook in small batches to avoid ingredients, particularly meats, stewing rather than frying (this makes meat tough and prevents brown-ing). Stir-fried vegetables should be crisp, but make sure they are sufficiently cooked. Two of the worst mistakes with stir-frying are overcooking meat and undercooking vegetables.

As stir-frying is so quick, have absolutely everything ready before you begin, including mixing sauces and thickeners, and all seasonings.

STEAMING

Steaming cooks food quite fast at very high heat and retains moisture and color in ingredients. To steam, heat water to simmering in a wok or the base of a steamer, then place food directly in steamer baskets or in shallow bowls or plates and place in the steamer. Cover tightly. Always open a steamer lid away from you to avoid burns, and take care when removing hot dishes. You can use a pair of steamer tongs to safely lift dishes from the steamer.

POACHING, SIMMERING AND BRAISING

Slow cooking draws seasonings and sauces deep into ingredients to create wonderfully rich and complex flavors.

Make sure ingredients are covered with liquid, and add more liquid during cooking if necessary. Cooking liquids can be reduced or thickened to serve as sauces. The term 'red cooking' refers to dishes cooked in a sauce flavored with soy sauce. 'Master stock' is a fragrant cooking liquid in which whole spices such as star anise, fennel, cinnamon and Sichuan pepper add spicy flavor highlights.

DEEP-FRYING

A mild vegetable or seed oil, or peanut oil is best for deep-frying – don't use olive oil, as it imparts a flavor that is not compatible with Chinese seasonings. Your wok is the best tool for deep-frying, as its sloping sides help prevent spill-over. A clever technique for testing if oil is hot enough for frying is to stand a wooden chopstick or the handle of a wooden spoon in the center of the wok. When a cloud of tiny bubbles gathers around the stick, the oil is ready. Alternatively, use a deep-frying or sugar thermometer to check that the oil is hot enough. If the oil is too hot, the outside of the food will crisp and darken before the inside is cooked. An easy way to quickly decrease oil temperature is to add a little extra unheated oil.

Before you begin to fry, arrange paper towels or a wire rack over a tray for draining the oil from the cooked food.

HOW TO 'ASIAN CUT' AN ONION

'Asian-cut' onion looks more attractive in a stir-fry than sliced or diced onion. Cut the top and bottom off the onion and peel. Insert the tip of a knife into the center of the onion from the top and cut downwards. Make another similar cut ¼ inch away and cut out the thin wedge. The layers will separate into curved pieces. Continue in this manner.

Essential Ingredients

Most common Chinese ingredients are now readily available from supermarkets and Asian food stores, and stocking up on the basic ingredients you will need is not expensive. Begin with small bottles of light soy sauce, rice vinegar, rice wine for cooking and sesame oil. Good-quality chicken stock, canned bamboo shoots, and corn starch or potato starch for coating and thickening sauces are essential, as is a neutral oil such as canola or sunflower seed oil (or the more flavorful peanut oil), and medium-grain white rice. You will also want to include a selection of your favorite dried noodles. Add white pepper, star anise, Sichuan peppercorns and sesame seeds to your spice rack.

Ready-to-use condiments like oyster sauce, hoisin sauce and bean pastes are best kept in the refrigerator, where they will last a long time. Fresh cilantro, chili peppers and spring onions are used so often it is worth growing your own in a herb garden. Fresh bean sprouts, ginger, bell peppers, acid-free cucumbers (such as English seedless), various Chinese greens, carrots, broccoli, green beans and onions complete the basic requirements for cooking Chinese food whenever you desire.

Salads & Cold Appetizers

While Chinese meals are not traditionally structured into courses, little plates of hot and cold appetizers are usually served as soon as guests are seated at the dining table. These dishes can be as simple as a plate of cold sliced meats, some crunchy nuts and tangy pickles, or a small salad in spicy dressing. The purpose is to excite the palate and stimulate the appetite.

As these dishes are small (usually just a few bites for each diner), they can be interesting and boldly flavored. Foods with unusual textures and flavors have particular appeal to the Chinese, who enjoy such delicacies as dried jellyfish, perhaps shredded into a salad, and pungent preserved eggs.

You may want to prepare several of these dishes if cooking for friends, or choose a single dish to start an at-home meal for the family.

< CHICKEN, CELERY & SPRING ONION SALAD (PAGE 14)

Chicken, Celery & Spring Onion Salad

SERVES 4–8

1 pound 2 ounces cold poached
   chicken breasts
3 celery stalks, finely sliced on a
   diagonal
6 spring onions (green parts
   only), roughly chopped
½ teaspoon Sichuan
   peppercorns

2½ tablespoons sesame oil
2 tablespoons light soy sauce
2 teaspoons oyster sauce or
   dark soy sauce
3 tablespoons chicken stock
   (page 242) or water

Tear the chicken into thin strips and place in a shallow bowl. Add the celery.

Place the spring-onion greens in a food processor or blender and chop until a paste forms.

Place the peppercorns in a small saucepan without oil, and toast over medium–high heat for 1 minute, then transfer to a mortar or spice grinder and grind finely.

In a large bowl, combine the spring-onion paste, ground pepper, sesame oil, light soy sauce, oyster sauce or dark soy sauce, and the chicken stock or water. Whisk until well combined.

Pour the sauce over the chicken and celery, and serve.

Bon Bon Chicken & Cucumber Salad

Bonbon ji

SERVES 6–10

1 white-poached chicken (page 164)

3 teaspoons sesame oil

2 English (seedless) cucumbers, cut into matchsticks

1 tablespoon sesame seeds, toasted

SESAME SAUCE

3 tablespoons chicken stock (page 242) or water

2 tablespoons tahini

2 tablespoons peanut oil

2 teaspoons sesame oil

1 tablespoon light soy sauce

1–2 teaspoons garlic chili bean paste

1½ teaspoons black Chinese vinegar or 1 teaspoon balsamic vinegar

½–1½ teaspoons granulated white sugar, to tase

Remove the chicken from its poaching liquid and place on a rack over a tray. Set aside for 1 hour until the meat has firmed and cooled. Brush the skin of the chicken with sesame oil and set aside for a few minutes. Debone the chicken and tear the meat into strips. Place in a medium-sized bowl.

Combine the sesame sauce ingredients in a small bowl, adding white sugar to taste. Add about half the sauce to the chicken and toss to coat. Arrange cucumbers on a platter, then scatter the chicken over the top. Sprinkle with sesame seeds. Serve with the remaining sauce in a bowl on the side.

Drunken Chicken

Zao zui ji

SERVES 6–10

1 (2 pound 7-ounce) chicken
1 tablespoon salt flakes (delicate
    finishing salt)
¾ cup rice wine
1½-inch piece fresh ginger,
    roughly chopped
2 spring onions, folded

1 teaspoon sugar
¾ teaspoon salt
pickled cucumber (page 26)
    and pickled ginger, to serve

Rinse and dry the chicken, then rub the skin with the salt flakes and sprinkle some inside the cavity. Also sprinkle 2 tablespoons of the rice wine inside the chicken. Push the ginger and folded spring onions into the cavity.

Place the chicken, breast facing up, in a steamer and steam for about 20 minutes, or until barely cooked (there may still be some pink around the bones). Transfer to a board and cover loosely with aluminum foil. Let rest for 10 minutes. Once cooled slightly, chop the chicken meat into bite-sized pieces and spread in a single layer in a shallow bowl.

Combine the remaining rice wine with the sugar and salt. Pour this mixture over the chicken and turn each piece to coat. Cover and refrigerate for about 24 hours, turning the chicken pieces several times.

Serve cold with pickled cucumber and pickled ginger.

Sliced Chicken with Sichuan-pepper Dressing

Jiao ma ji

SERVES 4–6

1–2 cold poached chicken
  breasts
¾ teaspoon Sichuan
  peppercorns
3 teaspoons sesame seeds
4 spring onions (green parts
  only), finely chopped

1½ tablespoons light soy sauce
1½ tablespoons sesame oil
1 teaspoon chili bean paste
water, to thin chili bean paste
salt, to taste

Slice the chicken thinly or tear it into small strips.

Place the Sichuan peppercorns and sesame seeds in a small fry pan without oil, and toast gently until seeds are golden and pepper fragrant (about 1½ minutes). Place into a spice grinder or mortar and grind coarsely.

In a bowl, combine the spring-onion greens, light soy sauce, sesame oil and chili bean paste. Add 3 tablespoons water and the pepper mixture and stir. Season with salt to taste.

Toss the sauce through the chicken. Serve cold.

Sliced Pork with Garlic Sauce

SERVES 4–6

$^1/_3$ quantity simmered pork
   (page 185)
3 tablespoons dark soy sauce
2–3 teaspoons chili oil
3 teaspoons finely chopped
   garlic

2 teaspoons granulated white
   sugar
$^1/_2$ teaspoon Chinese five-spice
   powder
2 teaspoons sesame oil

Very thinly slice the pork and arrange on a plate.

Combine the remaining ingredients in a small bowl and whisk to combine. (Or place in a screw-top jar and shake well.)

Pour the sauce into one or more small bowls and serve with the pork, for dipping.

✳ The pickled cucumber on page 26 goes well with this dish.

Tea Eggs
Cha dan

SERVES 5–10

10 eggs
cold water, to cover, boil and
   cool eggs
½ cup black tea leaves
2 star anise, roughly crushed
1 cinnamon stick, broken

2 teaspoons Chinese five-spice
   powder
3 tablespoons dark soy sauce
1 tablespoon salt
1 teaspoon sugar

Place the eggs in a saucepan with enough cold water to cover. Bring slowly to a boil, then reduce heat and simmer for 10 minutes, until hard boiled. Drain, and cool in cold water. Drain.

With the back of a teaspoon, tap the eggshells to crack them evenly all over, then return the eggs to the saucepan. Add the remaining ingredients and enough water to cover, and bring slowly to a boil. Reduce heat and simmer gently for about 2¼ hours, until the color has penetrated the cracks to stain the eggs in a marbled pattern and the eggs are delicately flavored with the spices. Remove eggs from water and cool.

Remove shells and cut the eggs into halves or wedges to serve.

The eggs will keep (unshelled) in the refrigerator for 5–6 days.

✽ Quail eggs can be prepared in the same way, but require only about 1¾ hours cooking.

Spiced Soy Beans

SERVES 4–8

1 pound soy beans in their pods
5 thin slices fresh ginger
warm water, to cover soy beans
½ teaspoon crushed Sichuan
   peppercorns
¾ teaspoon salt
2 teaspoons sesame oil

Place the soy beans in a saucepan and cover with warm water. Add the ginger, crushed peppercorns, salt and sesame oil, and bring to a boil. Reduce heat and simmer for 6–7 minutes.

Drain well and serve at room temperature.

❋ Soy beans (edamame) can sometimes be found fresh at specialty food markets, and are sold fresh and frozen in most Asian grocers.

Salt-boiled Peanuts
Lu hua sheng

SERVES 4–8

1½ cups large raw pink-skinned
   peanuts
1½ teaspoons salt
½ teaspoon fennel seeds
¾ teaspoon Sichuan
   peppercorns
water, to cover ingredients

Place all the ingredients in a saucepan and add enough water to cover. Bring to a boil, then reduce heat, cover, and simmer for about 20 minutes. Drain well.

Cool to room temperature before serving.

Sweet & Sour Cabbage

SERVES 6–8

14 ounces Chinese cabbage
  (wombok)
1 tablespoon salt
water, to rinse cabbage
1 fresh hot red chili pepper,
  deseeded and finely chopped
2 thin slices fresh ginger, finely
  shredded

2 tablespoons sesame oil
1 teaspoon Sichuan
  peppercorns
$^1/_3$ teaspoon fennel or caraway
  seeds
$2\frac{1}{2}$ tablespoons granulated
  white sugar
$2\frac{1}{2}$ tablespoons rice vinegar

Thinly slice the thick stems of the cabbage and roughly chop the leaves. Place in a bowl, add the salt and mix well. Cover and set aside for 3–4 hours, turning occasionally. Place cabbage into a colander to drain, pressing down to remove as much of the liquid as possible. Rinse lightly, if desired. Transfer to a bowl and mix in the red chili pepper and ginger.

In a small saucepan, heat the sesame oil with the peppercorns and fennel or caraway seeds for 1 minute over medium heat. Add the white sugar, rice vinegar and 2 tablespoons water, and bring barely to a boil. Pour the liquid over the cabbage and mix well. Cover and let marinate for 3–4 hours before serving.

This condiment can be stored, refrigerated, for at least 6 days.

Pickled Cucumber

3 English (seedless) cucumbers
$^1/_3$ cup white vinegar
$^1/_3$ cup granulated white sugar
2 teaspoons salt
2 teaspoons sesame oil
water, to prepare pickling
   liquid

1–2 teaspoons chili oil
   (optional)
1 fresh hot red chili pepper,
   deseeded and sliced

Cut the cucumbers in half lengthwise, then cut into slices about ½ inch thick. Place in a heatproof bowl.

Combine the vinegar, white sugar and salt with 3 tablespoons water in a small saucepan and bring to a boil. Immediately remove pan from the heat and pour the liquid over the cucumbers. Add the sesame oil, chilli oil (if using) and the sliced red chili pepper, mix well and set aside to cool.

Serve at room temperature.

Pickled Bean Sprouts

SERVES 4–8

9 ounces bean sprouts
  boiling and ice water, to
    cover bean sprouts and halt
    cooking
3 spring onions (green parts
  only), sliced
1 tablespoon rice vinegar
1 tablespoon light soy sauce
1 tablespoon sesame oil

1 teaspoon granulated white
  sugar
finely chopped red chili
  pepper, finely shredded
  ginger or chopped cilantro
  leaves (optional)

Place the bean sprouts in a bowl and cover with boiling water. Set aside for 1 minute, then drain. Return the sprouts to the bowl and immediately cover with ice water. Set aside for 5 minutes, then drain again. Mix the sprouts with the spring onion greens.

Whisk together the rice vinegar, light soy sauce, sesame oil and white sugar, then pour the dressing over the sprouts. Toss well and set aside for 20 minutes.

Before serving, adjust seasonings to taste, adding more vinegar or soy sauce if needed, and/or including some finely chopped red chili pepper, finely shredded ginger or chopped cilantro leaves.

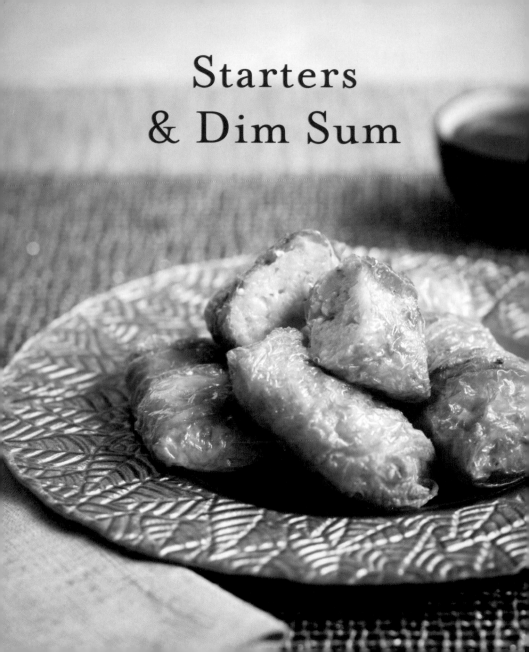

Starters
& Dim Sum

The buns, dumplings and other small snacks we call dim sum are delicious as a meal or snack, or can be served as a starter in a two- or three-course Chinese dinner. For a dim sum meal, offer several of these dishes, perhaps accompanied by a salad, sliced meat or pickle, and of course a pot of Chinese tea.

As a first course, any of these dishes can be served on its own, dressed up with a garnish of fresh herbs or a salad of small-leaf Asian greens. Decide on the main course first, then choose a starter with a different main ingredient and texture to complement it: try something crunchy before a soft noodle dish, or serve dumplings before a stir-fry.

Most deep-fried and steamed Chinese snacks are accompanied with small dishes of sauce or flavored salt for dipping, or you can offer plain light soy sauce or chili sauce. The Peking duck pancakes on page 154 also make a great starter.

< CRUNCHY PRAWN ROLLS (PAGE 30)

Crunchy Prawn Rolls

SERVES 4–6

¾ pounds raw (green) prawns, shelled and deveined

1¾ ounces fat bacon (side or streaky), finely diced

3 water chestnuts, finely chopped

1 thin slice fresh ginger, finely chopped

½ spring onion, finely chopped

1 egg white

½ teaspoon salt

1 teaspoon sesame oil

1½ tablespoons cornstarch, plus more to form paste

2–3 sheets dried bean-curd skin, soaked in water for 2 minutes

water, to form paste

vegetable oil for deep-frying

sweet and sour sauce (page 236) or Sichuan pepper–salt (page 240), to serve

Chop the prawns in a food processor or blender, then combine in a bowl with the bacon, water chestnuts, ginger, spring onion, egg white, salt, sesame oil and corn starch.

Drain the bean-curd skins and pat dry with paper towels. Cut into 7-inch squares and place a spoonful of filling in the center of each square. Fold in the sides, then fold over to make flat bundles. Make a thin paste with cornstarch and water, and spread a little on the end of each wrapper to adhere.

Heat the vegetable oil to about 325° F. Fry the prawn rolls, a few at a time, for 1–1½ minutes, until golden brown. Drain on paper towels.

Serve hot with sweet and sour sauce or pepper–salt for dipping.

Steamed Prawns with Soy–Chili Dipping Sauce

SERVES 6–8

1 tablespoon salt

ice and hot water, to chill and simmer prawns

1 pound 10 ounces medium-sized raw (green) prawns, in their shells

ice water and hot water, to chill and simmer prawns

3 tablespoons light soy sauce

3 tablespoons dark soy sauce

1 teaspoon granulated white sugar

$^1/_3$ cup cooked oil

1 small fresh hot red chili pepper, deseeded and chopped

2 thin slices fresh ginger, finely chopped

1 clove garlic, finely chopped

$^1/_2$ spring onion, finely chopped

Dissolve the salt in a large bowl of ice water, then add the prawns and set aside for 15 minutes.

Fill the bottom of a steamer with hot water and bring to a boil, then reduce to a high simmer.

Drain the prawns and spread them in the steamer basket. Set the basket in the steamer and steam for 8–10 minutes, until prawns are pink and firm.

Combine the remaining ingredients in a bowl, then divide the sauce among several small dishes for dipping.

Place the steamed prawns onto a serving plate and serve at once, with the dipping sauce alongside.

Crisp-fried Prawns with Sichuan Pepper–Salt

SERVES 4

1 pound 2 ounce small raw
   (green) prawns, in their
   shells
3 tablespoons cornstarch
vegetable oil for deep-frying
2 tablespoons sesame oil
2 spring onions, very finely
   chopped

2 cloves garlic, very finely
   chopped
1 small fresh hot red chili
   pepper, deseeded and
   chopped
1½ tablespoons Sichuan
   pepper–salt (page 240)

Use kitchen scissors to trim off the prawn legs and the sharp point of the head.
Coat prawns lightly with cornstarch.

Heat vegetable oil in a wok to 375°F. Fry the prawns, stirring slowly, for about
2 minutes, until well cooked and crunchy – the shells should be pink and crisp.
Remove with a wire skimmer and drain on paper towels. Pour the vegetable oil
out of the wok.

Add the sesame oil, spring onions, garlic and red chili pepper to the wok and
stir-fry for about 1 minute, until crisp. Return prawns to the wok and add 1 tablespoon of the pepper–salt (use remaining salt to garnish). Toss over high heat until
prawns are evenly coated.

Serve at once, sprinkled with the remaining pepper–salt.

Golden Prawn Balls

SERVES 4–6

10½ ounces shelled raw (green) prawns, deveined

1¾ ounces fatty pork (such as pork belly), diced

1 egg, separated

2 teaspoons sesame oil

1 teaspoon finely chopped fresh ginger

¼ cup very finely chopped water chestnuts

2 teaspoons cornstarch

salt and ground white pepper

water, to beat with egg yolk

2 cups fresh breadcrumbs

vegetable oil for deep-frying

sweet and sour sauce (page 236) or Sichuan pepper–salt (page 240), to serve

Place prawns, fatty pork, egg white and sesame oil in a blender or food processor and blend to a slightly coarse paste. Place mixture into a bowl and stir in the ginger, water chestnuts, cornstarch and a generous pinch each of salt and ground white pepper. Mix thoroughly. Use wet hands to form the mixture into walnut-sized balls.

Add 1 tablespoon water to the egg yolk and beat well. Dip the balls in the egg mixture, then roll them in breadcrumbs to coat.

Heat the vegetable oil to 350°F. Fry the prawn balls, in two batches, for 1½–2 minutes, until golden brown and cooked through. Drain on paper towels.

Serve hot with sweet and sour sauce or Sichuan pepper–salt for dipping.

Fried Oysters with Five-spice Salt

SERVES 2–4

12 large fresh oysters on the
  half shell
¾-inch piece fresh ginger
cold water, to mix with ginger
1 teaspoon rice wine
½ cup cornstarch
½ cup all-purpose flour, plus
  extra for dusting
¹/₃ teaspoon ground white
  pepper
ice-cold water, to make batter
2 egg whites
vegetable oil for deep-frying
five-spice salt (page 246),
  to serve

Remove oysters from their shells and place in a dish.

Grate the ginger onto a clean piece of cheesecloth and add 2 teaspoons cold water. Squeeze the ginger juice over the oysters and add the rice wine. Marinate in the refrigerator for 15 minutes.

Rinse and drain the oyster shells and place on a baking sheet in a low oven to warm while you prepare the oysters.

In a bowl, combine the cornstarch, all-purpose flour and ground white pepper, and add enough ice-cold water to make a thick batter, taking care not to overmix it. Beat the egg whites to soft peaks, then fold into the batter.

Heat vegetable oil in a wok to 350°F.

Dust the oysters lightly with extra all-purpose flour. When the vegetable oil is hot, dip the oysters into the batter, one by one, coating generously. Slip oysters carefully into the vegetable oil and fry for about 1½ minutes, until lightly golden and crisp. Remove with a slotted spoon, drain, then place each oyster onto a warmed shell.

Serve at once with five-spice salt for dipping.

Squid Skewers with Sweet & Sour Sauce

SERVES 4–6

1–2 large squid tubes (about 10½ ounces in total)

2 teaspoons freshly squeezed lemon juice

1 clove garlic, crushed

½ teaspoon ground chili powder (optional)

½ teaspoon salt

water, to marinate squid

½ cup cornstarch

2 tablespoons rice flour or tapioca flour

vegetable oil for deep-frying

sweet and sour sauce (page 236), to serve

Cut each squid tube along one side and open out. Using a sharp knife, score the inner surface in a cross-hatch pattern. Cut into 2-inch squares.

Combine the lemon juice, garlic, chili powder (if using) and salt in a bowl with 2 tablespoons water. Add the squid and marinate for 20 minutes, turning several times. Drain, and dry on paper towels.

Mix the cornstarch and rice or tapioca flour in a plastic bag, add squid and shake to coat. Place into a colander and shake off excess coating. Thread two pieces of squid onto each skewer.

Heat vegetable oil to 375°F and fry the squid skewers, in batches, for 15–30 seconds only – overcooking will make the squid tough and rubbery. Remove and drain on paper towels.

Serve at once, with sweet and sour sauce for dipping.

Sang Choy Bau

MAKES 8–12 (SERVES 4–6)

8–12 iceberg lettuce leaves

5 dried shiitake mushrooms, soaked in hot water for 25 minutes

2 tablespoons vegetable oil

1 tablespoon sesame oil

1 pound 7 ounces minced pork or chicken (coarsely ground)

2 spring onions, finely chopped

3/8-inch piece fresh ginger, finely chopped

3½ ounce water chestnuts, finely chopped

2 dried Chinese sausages or 1 slice bacon, finely diced

2 tablespoons hoisin sauce, plus extra to serve

1 tablespoon light soy sauce

salt and freshly ground black pepper

2½ teaspoons cornstarch

water, to mix cornstarch

2 tablespoons chopped cilantro or mint, for garnish

Trim the lettuce leaves into round cups and set aside.

Drain the mushrooms and squeeze out excess water. Trim off tough stems and finely dice the caps.

Heat the oils in a wok and stir-fry the minced pork or chicken and spring onions over high heat until the meat is lightly browned. Add the ginger, mushrooms, water chestnuts, and sausage or bacon, and stir-fry for 1½–2 minutes, until meat is well cooked.

Season the mixture with the hoisin sauce, soy sauce, and salt and pepper to taste.

Mix the cornstarch with ½ cup water and pour into the wok. Stir over high heat until the mixture thickens and binds together.

Spoon the mixture into the lettuce cups to serve. Garnish with cilantro or mint and serve with a little extra hoisin sauce.

✳ Chinese sausage is available in Asian markets, mostly vaccum-packed.

Pot-sticker Dumplings
Wor tip

MAKES 36 (SERVES 6–8)

vegetable oil, for shallow-frying

3 tablespoons chicken stock
(page 242) or water

light soy sauce or Chinese black
vinegar, to serve

DUMPLING DOUGH

1¾ cups all-purpose flour

⅓ teaspoon salt

7 fluid ounces boiling water

a few drops of vegetable oil

FILLING

13 ounce skinless pork belly,
diced

2½ ounces bamboo shoots or
water chestnuts, very finely
chopped

2 ounces Chinese cabbage
(wombok), very finely
chopped

4 garlic chives, very finely
chopped

2 teaspoons light soy sauce

1 teaspoon rice wine

salt and ground white pepper

½ teaspoon sesame oil

To make the dumpling dough, sift the all-purpose flour and salt into a bowl. Make a well in the center and pour in the boiling water. Mix with the handle of a wooden spoon until the dough comes together, then place onto a work surface and knead gently for 1 minute. Shape into a smooth ball. Sprinkle a few drops of vegetable oil over the surface of the dough, then cover with the upturned bowl. Set aside for about 30 minutes. ❯

To make the filling, place the pork in a food processor or blender and grind to a smooth paste. Transfer to a bowl and mix with the remaining filling ingredients.

Knead the dough for 6–8 minutes, then roll it into a sausage shape and cut into three equal-sized pieces. Keep two pieces covered with a damp cloth while working with the third piece. Cut the piece of dough into 12 equal-sized pieces. Roll out each small piece into a thin 3-inch round. Place a spoonful of the filling slightly off-center on each round. Pleat the edge of the larger side, fold it over the filling and press it onto the unpleated edge to create dumplings with one flat side and one crimped side. Tap the bottom gently against the worktop to flatten. Repeat with the two remaining pieces of dough to make 24 more dumplings.

Generously oil a large cast-iron or non-stick pan and place over medium–high heat. Arrange the dumplings side by side in the pan (in batches if necessary) and fry for about 2 minutes. Carefully pour off excess oil, then add the chicken stock or water, cover, and steam for about 2 minutes. Uncover and simmer gently for about 3 minutes more, until the liquid is evaporated and dumpling skins are tender.

Place dumplings onto a plate. (Or for crisp dumplings, turn the dumplings over in the pan, add a little more vegetable oil and fry on medium–high heat until golden brown.) Serve with light soy sauce or Chinese black vinegar for dipping.

✳ Use store-bought dumpling wrappers (gou gees) if you're short of time.

Crunchy Pork with Five-spice Salt

SERVES 4

2 large pork chops (about
  1 pound in total)
1 tablespoon light soy sauce
2 teaspoons sesame oil
2 teaspoons rice wine
1 egg white, well beaten

cornstarch, for coating
vegetable oil for deep-frying
2–3 tablespoons five-spice salt
  (page 246)

Using a Chinese cleaver or heavy knife, chop the pork chops into pieces about 2 inches × ¾ inches. Place in a bowl and add the light soy sauce, sesame oil, rice wine and egg white, and mix well. Set aside to marinate for 20 minutes.

Drain the pork, then coat with cornstarch, shaking off excess.

Heat the vegetable oil in a wok to 350°F. Fry the pork, in two batches, for 2½–3 minutes, until crisp, golden brown and cooked through. Drain well on paper towels.

Reheat the oil to 375°F and quickly fry all the pork at once for about 30 seconds. Drain on paper towels.

Arrange pork on a serving plate, with the five-spice salt in a bowl for dipping.

Steamed Pork Buns

Chao shiu bao

MAKES 10

DOUGH

1½ cups all-purpose flour

2¼ teaspoons baking powder

⅓ teaspoon superfine (bar) sugar

water, to prepare dough

2½ fluid ounces lukewarm milk

about 1½ tablespoons vegetable oil, plus extra for sautéing

FILLING

1 spring onion, finely chopped

2 teaspoons vegetable oil

⅔ cup diced red roast pork (page 179)

1 tablespoon oyster sauce

1 teaspoon granulated white sugar

ground white pepper

a few drops of sesame oil

3 tablespoons chicken stock (page 242) or water

1 teaspoon cornstarch

To prepare the dough, combine the flour, baking powder and superfine sugar on a clean work surface and make a well in the center. Add the milk and gently work the flour into the liquid, adding up to 2½ tablespoons water and 1½ tablespoons vegetable oil, as needed, to make a soft but not sticky dough. Knead for about 10 minutes, until elastic, sprinkling the dough with flour if sticky and moistening your hands with water and oil if it is dry. **>**

Cover the dough with a damp cloth and set aside for 1 hour.

To make the filling, sauté the spring onion in vegetable oil for about 1 minute, until soft and translucent. Add the pork and remaining ingredients (except chicken stock or water and cornstarch) and stir-fry until well mixed. Add the chicken stock or water and cornstarch, and cook gently to bind the filling.

Cut ten 2¼-inch rounds of parchment (baking) paper and set aside.

Roll the dough into a sausage shape and cut into ten equal-sized pieces. Press out each piece with your fingers to make a round about 5 inches in diameter. Place a spoonful of filling in the center and bring the dough up around it to enclose, twisting and pinching the edges to seal. Set each bun on a round of parchment paper, with the joined edges facing up.

Place buns in a steamer, allowing space for each to expand, and steam for 15–18 minutes, until soft and spongy. Serve at once.

Steamed Beef Balls

Jiu zi zheng

SERVES 4

3 outer leaves of Chinese
   cabbage (wombok), roughly
   chopped
boiling salted water, to blanch
   cabbage
10½ ounces lean beef, diced
1¾ ounces pork fat, diced

1 tablespoon light soy sauce
1 egg white
1½ teaspoons sesame oil
pinch of ground white pepper
simmering water, to steam beef
   balls
Chinese black vinegar, to serve

Blanch the cabbage in boiling salted water, then drain and spread in a steamer basket.

Place the beef, pork fat, light soy sauce, egg white, sesame oil and ground white pepper in a blender or food processor, and grind to a smooth, sticky paste. With wet hands, form the mixture into walnut-sized balls and arrange on the cabbage.

Set the basket in the steamer over simmering water, and steam for about 6 minutes.

Serve hot, in the basket, with Chinese black vinegar for dipping.

Spring Rolls

Chun gun

MAKES 20

4 large dried shiitake
  mushrooms, soaked in hot
  water for 25 minutes
7 ounce pork fillet
3 cups vegetable oil, for frying
3 thin slices fresh ginger, finely
  shredded
1¾ ounces garlic chives, cut
  into ⅜-inch pieces
3 ounces bean sprouts
2 teaspoons soy sauce

1 teaspoon rice wine
a few drops of sesame oil
salt and ground white pepper
20 small square spring-roll
  wrappers
water or beaten egg, to brush
  wrappers
sweet and sour sauce (page
  236) or sweet chili sauce,
  to serve

Drain the mushrooms and squeeze out excess water. Trim off the tough stems and finely slice the mushroom caps.

Thinly slice the pork, then stack the slices and cut into fine shreds.

Heat 2 tablespoons vegetable oil in a wok over high heat and stir-fry the mushrooms and ginger for 30 seconds. Add the pork shreds and stir-fry for about 1 minute, until they turn white. Add the garlic chives, bean sprouts, soy sauce, rice wine and sesame oil, and season to taste with salt and pepper.

Spread the filling on a plate to cool.

Place a portion of filling in the center of each spring-roll wrapper. Roll one corner over the filling, shaping the filling into a log, then fold the two sides in and roll up the log. Brush the end of the wrapper with water or beaten egg white to make sure it sticks down.

Heat vegetable oil for deep-frying to 350°F. Fry the spring rolls, in two or three batches, for about 1½ minutes, until golden brown.

Serve with sweet and sour sauce or sweet chili sauce for dipping.

Soups,
Soup Noodles
& Steamboats

Hardly a day goes by in a Chinese home without soup being served. Soup noodles are happily eaten for breakfast, enjoyed as a morning or afternoon snack, and anticipated as a late-night pick-me-up. A bowl of soup, with or without noodles, is a filling, nutritious and satisfying snack at any time of the day.

At meal time, soup is usually served midway through a Chinese menu, rather than at the beginning, but any of these delicious soups can be served as a starter for a family meal or dinner party.

Chinese soup is usually garnished simply, with a sprinkle of chopped spring-onion greens or cilantro leaves. But for some extra crunch or punch, you could try serving them with sliced fresh chili peppers, roasted peanuts or crispy fried noodles.

< WONTON SOUP (PAGE 54)

Wonton Soup
Huntun tang

SERVES 6

WONTONS

4½ ounces minced (coarsely ground) pork

8 ounce shelled and deveined raw (green) prawns

¼ cup finely chopped water chestnuts or bamboo shoots

8 garlic chives or 3 spring onions (white parts only), finely chopped

1 teaspoon light soy sauce

½ teaspoon salt

1 packet wonton wrappers

1 egg white, lightly beaten

salted water, to cook wontons

SOUP

5 cups chicken stock (page 242)

2 thin slices fresh ginger, finely shredded

3 spring onions (green parts only)

3 ounces baby spinach, Chinese water spinach, or watercress

2–3 teaspoons light soy sauce, plus extra to serve

2–3 teaspoons sesame oil

chili oil (optional)

To make the wonton filling, place the minced pork and prawns in a food processor or blender and grind to a coarse paste. Add the water chestnuts or bamboo shoots, garlic chives or spring onions, soy sauce and salt, and grind in the food processor or blender or squeeze through your fingers until the mixture binds together.

Place a teaspoon of filling in the center of each wonton wrapper, brush the edges with egg white, then fold over to make a triangle. Bring the two outer points together and pinch to form the wonton shape.

Bring a large saucepan of salted water to a boil, add the wontons and bring back to a boil. Cook for about 3 minutes or until the wontons float to the surface. Scoop out the wontons with a slotted spoon and divide among six bowls.

Bring the chicken stock and ginger to a boil, then add half spring-onion greens, spinach leaves, light soy sauce and sesame oil. Simmer for 2 minutes.

Pour the soup over the wontons, garnish with the remaining spring onions, and serve with extra light soy sauce and chili oil (if using) for drizzling.

Prawn & Green Vegetable Soup

SERVES 4

4 baby bok choy or Chinese
   mustard greens, quartered
   lengthways
boiling water, to blanch
   vegetables
1 quart 2 ounces chicken stock
   (page 242)
1 spring onion, finely chopped
1 teaspoon finely shredded
   ginger

2 teaspoons rice wine
   (optional)
16 medium-sized raw (green)
   prawns, butterflied but tails
   left on
1 teaspoon sesame oil or chili
   oil (optional)
salt and ground white pepper
light soy sauce

Blanch the vegetables in boiling water, and drain at once.

Combine the chicken stock, spring onion, ginger and rice wine (if using) in a saucepan and bring to a boil. Add the prawns and vegetables, and simmer for 2–3 minutes. Sprinkle in sesame or chili oil, if desired, and season with salt, ground white pepper and a few teaspoons of light soy sauce.

Chicken & Corn Soup
Ji yumi geng

SERVES 3–5

½ pound chicken breast fillets, very finely diced
salt and ground white pepper
½ teaspoon sesame oil
3 cups chicken stock
1 (8-ounce) can creamed corn
1 tablespoon cornstarch
cold water, to mix with cornstarch
2 eggs, beaten
2–3 teaspoons chopped fresh cilantro or spring-onion greens, for garnish

Season the chicken breast fillet with ½ teaspoon salt, ¼ teaspoon ground white pepper and the sesame oil. Mix well. Marinate for 20 minutes.

Bring the chicken stock to a boil in a medium-sized saucepan. Add the chicken and creamed corn, and bring back to a boil. Simmer for 2 minutes.

Mix the cornstarch with 3 tablespoons cold water, then stir into the soup. Bring soup to a boil again, stirring, then reduce heat and simmer gently until the soup thickens (about 5 minutes). Season to taste with salt and ground white pepper.

Remove pan from the heat. Drizzle in the beaten eggs, so they set in thin strands in the soup. Return pan to the heat and gently reheat the soup.

Serve garnished with cilantro or spring-onion greens.

Chicken & Rice-noodle Soup

SERVES 4–6

5 cups chicken stock (page 242)

2 chicken thigh fillets, diced

3 spring onions, chopped (white and green parts kept separate)

2 thin slices fresh ginger, finely shredded

½ cup bamboo shoots or carrots cut into matchsticks

salt and ground white pepper

3 teaspoons light soy sauce, plus extra to serve

7 ounces dried rice-stick noodles

boiling unsalter water, to cook noodles

Combine the chicken stock, chicken, white parts of the spring onion, ginger, and bamboo shoots or carrots in a saucepan and bring to a boil. Reduce heat and simmer for 5–6 minutes. Season to taste with salt and ground white pepper, and add light soy sauce.

Cook the rice-stick noodles in boiling unsalted water for about 3½ minutes, until softened. Drain.

Divide the rice-stick noodles among bowls, then evenly distribute the chicken and vegetables, and ladle the soup over. Garnish with spring-onion greens and serve with extra light soy sauce.

Egg Thread Soup
Danhua tang

SERVES 4

1 quart 2 ounces chicken stock
  (page 242)
3 slices fresh ginger, finely
  shredded
1 teaspoon sesame oil
2–3 teaspoons light soy sauce

salt and ground white pepper
4 eggs, well beaten
1 spring onion (green part
  only), finely sliced, for
  garnish

Combine the chicken stock and ginger in a saucepan, bring to a boil, then reduce heat and simmer for 1 minute. Add the sesame oil and light soy sauce, and season lightly with salt and ground white pepper.

Remove pan from the heat and add the beaten eggs in a thin stream, so they set in fine strands in the soup. When the eggs have set, return pan to the heat and gently warm the soup.

Serve garnished with spring-onion greens.

Chinese Cabbage & Oyster Mushroom Soup

2 slices smoked bacon, finely
   chopped
9 ounces Chinese cabbage
   (wombok), chopped
3 cups chicken stock (page 242)
8 oyster mushrooms, cut in
   half
1 tablespoon light soy sauce
salt and ground white pepper

Sauté the bacon in a medium-sized saucepan, without oil, until crisp. Add the Chinese cabbage and stir-fry until it wilts. Pour in the chicken stock, then add the mushrooms and light soy sauce, and bring to a boil.

Simmer the soup for about 8 minutes, until the cabbage is tender. Season to taste with salt and ground white pepper, and serve.

Sichuan Hot & Sour Soup

Suan la tang

SERVES 4–6

1 quart 2 ounces chicken stock (page 242)

3 ounces finely shredded lean pork

3 ounces finely shredded chicken breast

3 ounces shelled and deveined raw (green) prawns, halved lengthwise

3 ounces firm tofu, diced

3–5 ounces fresh Asian mushrooms, including wood ear fungus, sliced

2 spring onions, finely sliced

5 thin slices fresh ginger, finely shredded

2 tablespoons Chinese black vinegar, plus extra to serve

1½ teaspoons dark soy sauce

1–2 teaspoons chili oil

salt and ground white pepper

½–1 teaspoon white granulated sugar

1½ tablespoons cornstarch

cold water, to mix in cornstarch

2 eggs, beaten

Bring the stock to a boil in a large saucepan or wok. Add all of the ingredients (except seasonings, cornstarch water and eggs). Bring to a boil and simmer for 5 minutes, then season with salt, pepper and sugar.

Mix the cornstarch with ⅓ cup cold water, and stir into the soup. Simmer, stirring occasionally, until the soup thickens. Remove from the heat. Add the eggs in a thin stream, so they sets in fine strands.

Serve hot, with extra Chinese black vinegar.

Mushrooms, Tofu & Thick Noodles in Chicken Soup

SERVES 4–6

2 pound 3 ounces fresh chicken necks or bones

12 small dried shiitake mushrooms

¾-inch piece fresh ginger, cut in half

4 spring onions, chopped (white and green parts kept separate)

water, to cook chicken

7 ounces fresh thick wheat-flour noodles or udon noodles

4 ounces silken tofu, diced

salt and ground white pepper

3 teaspoons light soy sauce

Place the chicken necks or bones in a saucepan and add the mushrooms, ginger and white parts of the spring onions. Pour in 7 cups water. Bring to a boil, then reduce heat to very low and simmer gently, uncovered, for 1 hour, skimming the surface from time to time.

Pick the mushrooms out of the soup and trim off the woody stems. Place the caps aside. Strain the soup into a clean saucepan.

Pour hot water over the fresh noodles and gently untangle using chopsticks. Drain. Divide the noodles, tofu, mushrooms and spring-onion greens evenly among serving bowls. Season the broth with salt, ground white pepper and the light soy sauce, then ladle into the bowls.

Duck & Shiitake Mushroom Soup with Egg Noodles

SERVES 6

1 Chinese roast duck carcass, including neck

1–2 Chinese roast duck legs

8 dried shiitake mushrooms, soaked in ¾ cup hot water for 25 minutes

2 star anise

1-inch piece cinnamon stick

water, to cook duck carcass

2 tablespoons dark soy sauce

2 bundles dried thin egg noodles

lightly salted boiling water, to cook noodles

2–3 ounces baby spinach leaves

salt

ground white pepper or Sichuan pepper

hoisin or light soy sauce

Place the duck carcass, neck and legs in a large saucepan. Strain the mushroom soaking liquid into the pan, and add the mushrooms, star anise, cinnamon stick and 5 cups water. Bring to a boil, then reduce heat to very low, add the dark soy sauce and simmer for about 45 minutes, skimming occasionally.

In another saucepan, cook the egg noodles in lightly salted boiling water for 6 minutes, or until tender. Drain.

Divide noodles and spinach leaves equally among six bowls.

Remove the duck carcass and neck from the soup. Transfer the duck legs to a cutting board, remove the skin and bones, and shred the meat. Divide the meat evenly among the bowls.

Strain the soup into a clean saucepan and season to taste with salt, ground white or Sichuan pepper and hoisin or light soy sauce.

Ladle soup into the bowls and serve.

Sichuan Hotpot
Si chuan huo guo

SERVES 6

HOTPOT STOCK

2⅔ quarts beef or chicken stock
   (page 242)
4 thick slices fresh ginger
1½ tablespoons salted black
   beans
4–24 hot dried chilies (4–8
   makes a pleasantly spicy
   stock)
3 tablespoons peanut oil
1–3 tablespoons chili bean
   paste
2 tablespoons rice wine
½–1 tablespoon granulated
   white sugar

DIPS

sesame oil
light soy sauce mixed with
   crushed garlic
Chinese five-spice powder or
   Sichuan pepper–salt
   (page 240)

HOTPOT INGREDIENTS

**Assemble a variety of these
raw ingredients on platters,
allowing 7–9 ounces in total
per person:**
sliced chicken breast
pineapple-cut squid, cut into
   2-inch squares
diced firm tofu
thinly sliced beef or lamb
fresh or dried shiitake
   mushrooms (soak dried
   mushrooms in hot water for
   25 minutes)
oyster or button mushrooms,
   whole or cut in half
small Chinese vegetables such
   as baby bok choy
sliced zucchini
small florets of broccoli or
   cauliflower
raw (green) prawns, shelled and
   deveined >

Place a steamboat (Chinese fondue or hot pot, or wok set over a portable gas cooker) in the center of the dining table. Add all stock ingredients to the wok and bring to a boil.

Place the dips in separate small bowls for each diner.

Using wooden chopsticks or bamboo skewers, each diner submerges their chosen ingredients in the stock until cooked, then dips them into the sesame oil, light garlic soy, Chinese five-spice powder or sichuan pepper-salt before eating.

Small bowls of the cooking broth can be served as a soup to finish the meal if desired.

✳ Salted black beans are also called Chinese fermented black beans.

✳ This dish can be served searing hot or pleasantly spicy, as preferred.

Crab Noodle Soup

7 ounces crab meat

²/₃ teaspoon grated ginger

4 ounces dried thin egg
noodles

lightly salted boiling water, to
cook noodles

2 egg whites

1½ teaspoons salt

1 teaspoon sesame oil

2 teaspoons light soy sauce

3½ cups chicken stock (page
242)

1¹/₃ tablespoons cornstarch

ground white pepper

1–2 tablespoons chopped
cilantro or spring-onion
greens, for garnish

Pick over the crab meat to remove any fragments of shell and break up any lumps. Mix with the ginger.

Cook the egg noodles in lightly salted boiling water until just tender. Drain.

Lightly whisk the egg whites with ½ teaspoon of the salt and sesame oil.

Combine the light soy sauce, chicken stock, cornstarch, ground white peper and remaining salt in a saucepan, and bring to a boil, stirring. Reduce heat and simmer for about 2 minutes, until slightly thickened. Stir in the crab and egg noodles, and check for seasoning. Simmer for 1–2 minutes. Remove from the heat and drizzle in the egg whites so they set in fine strands.

Serve garnished with cilantro or spring-onion greens.

Mongolian Steamboat
Shuan yang rou

SERVES 4

water, to fill steamboat

1 pound 2 ounces lean lamb,
   sliced paper thin

1–2 bunches baby bok choy,
   quartered lengthwise

1–2 small bundles (1½–3
   ounces) bean-thread noodles

2 tablespoons finely shredded
   ginger

hot water, to soak noodles

2–3 tablespoons finely chopped
   spring onion

1½ tablespoons light soy sauce

DIPPING SAUCE

2 teaspoons dark soy sauce

2 tablespoons light soy sauce

1 tablespoon rice wine

¼–1 teaspoon chili oil

2 teaspoons sesame oil

1 tablespoon peanut oil

1½ tablespoons red or black
   Chinese vinegar

2–3 teaspoons granulated white
   sugar

Place a steamboat in the center of the dining table. Fill with water and bring to a gentle simmer.

Arrange lamb and bok choy on serving platters. Soak the bean-thread noodles in hot water until softened.

Add half the ginger and spring onion to the water in the steamboat, and pour in the light soy sauce.

Drain the bean-thread noodles and place on a plate.

Whisk together the dipping sauce ingredients, adding sugar to taste, and divide among four small bowls. Add the remaining ginger and spring onion to the bowls of sauce.

At the table, diners use wooden chopsticks to place slivers of lamb in the stock to cook for a few seconds, then dip them into the sauce before eating.

Once all the lamb has been eaten, the bok choy and noodles are cooked in the stock and served as a soup.

✷ If you do not have a steamboat (Chinese fondue or hot pot), you can use an electric wok or a saucepan set over a portable gas cooker.

Stir-fries

Stir-frying is one of the healthiest and easiest ways to cook. Begin with a wok, a wok spatula and a good source of heat. Most gas stoves now have a wok burner. There are also induction stoves designed for wok use, and with a flat-bottomed wok good stir-fries can be achieved on an electric ring or hotplate. Electric woks also work well.

Stir-frying requires high heat. Heat the wok before adding the oil, and heat the oil before tossing in the ingredients: this way the ingredients won't stick to the pan and the food cooks quickly. It's important to have all ingredients, sauces and seasonings ready to go before you heat the wok. It's also wise to start the rice before you begin to stir-fry.

Never overload the wok — cooking too much at once results in soggy vegetables and tough meat. To avoid this, cook in small batches, and then return everything to the wok at the end and toss together to heat through.

< CHICKEN, ALMOND & VEGETABLE STIR-FRY (PAGE 78)

Chicken, Almond & Vegetable Stir-fry

SERVES 3–4

10½ ounces chicken breast fillets, thinly sliced

2 tablespoons light soy sauce

1½ teaspoons cornstarch

¾ cup chicken stock (page 242)

1 cup vegetable oil for frying

½ cup blanched almonds

8 small broccoli florets

8 small cauliflower florets

1 small onion, 'Asian cut' (see page 10)

1 small carrot, sliced on a diagonal

2 celery stalks, sliced on a diagonal

½ small zucchini, sliced

water, to steam vegetable

2 thin slices fresh ginger, finely shredded

½ teaspoon granulated white sugar

1 teaspoon rice wine

salt and ground white pepper

steamed white rice or cooked noodles, to serve

Place the chicken in a bowl and add 2 teaspoons of the light soy sauce and ½ teaspoon of the cornstarch. Mix well and set aside to marinate for about 10 minutes.

Stir the remaining cornstarch into the chicken stock. Set aside.

Heat the vegetable oil in a wok and fry the almonds for about 45 seconds, until lightly golden. Drain on paper towels and set aside.

Carefully pour all but 1 tablespoon vegetable oil from the wok into a bowl and reserve. Reheat the wok over high heat. Stir-fry the vegetables for 30 seconds, then add 3 tablespoons water, cover the wok and steam the vegetables for 2 minutes. Transfer to a plate.

Wipe out the wok with paper towels and reheat with another 2 tablespoons of the vegetable oil. Stir-fry half the chicken with the shredded ginger for 30 seconds. Transfer to a plate. Stir-fry the remaining chicken for 30 seconds.

Return all the chicken and the vegetables to the wok, and add the remaining light soy sauce, the sugar and rice wine. Stir-fry for 30 seconds, then season to taste with salt and ground white pepper.

Pour the chicken and cornstarch mixture into the wok and continue to simmer, stirring, until the sauce thickens. Stir in the almonds.

Serve at once with steamed white rice, or over cooked noodles.

Chicken with Mushrooms, Spring Onions & Ginger
Ji gu chao

SERVES 2–4

14 ounces chicken breast fillets

2 tablespoons light soy sauce

2 teaspoons rice wine

½ teaspoon granulated white sugar

1½ teaspoons cornstarch

6 large dried shiitake mushrooms, soaked in hot water for 25 minutes

⅔ cup chicken stock (page 242)

⅓ cup vegetable oil

4 spring onions, cut into 1¼-inch lengths

3 thin slices fresh ginger, finely shredded

salt and ground white pepper

steamed white rice, to serve

Slice the chicken thinly, then cut into ¾-inch × 1½-inch strips. Place in a bowl and add ½ teaspoon of the light soy sauce, the rice wine, sugar and ½ teaspoon of the cornstarch. Mix well and marinate for 20 minutes.

Drain the mushrooms, squeezing out excess water, then trim off the tough stems and cut the mushroom caps into quarters. Set aside.

Stir the remaining cornstarch into the chicken stock and set aside.

Heat the vegetable oil in a wok over high heat. Stir-fry the chicken, in two batches, for about 1½ minutes, until pale and firm, then set aside on a plate.

Stir-fry the mushrooms, spring onions and ginger for about 45 seconds. Add the remaining light soy sauce and return the chicken to the wok. Pour in the chicken stock and cornstarch mixutre and stir over high heat until the sauce thickens and coats the chicken and vegetables. Season to taste with salt and ground white pepper.

Serve at once with steamed white rice.

✳ Fresh shiitake or oyster mushrooms, or sliced canned straw mushrooms, can replace the dried mushrooms.

Satay Chicken Stir-fry
Sa te ji

SERVES 3–4

12 ounces chicken breast fillets, very thinly sliced
1 teaspoon finely grated ginger
1½ tablespoons light soy sauce
1½ teaspoons cornstarch
½ cup chicken stock (page 242)
3 tablespoons satay sauce
9 ounces bean sprouts

boiling water, to blanch bean sprouts
2½ tablespoons vegetable oil
2 spring onions, finely shredded (white and green parts kept separate)
1–2 fresh hot red chili peppers, deseeded and finely shredded

Place the chicken in a bowl with the ginger, 2 teaspoons light soy sauce and ½ teaspoon cornstarch. Mix well and marinate for 20 minutes. Combine the remaining light soy sauce and cornstarch with the chicken stock and satay sauce.

Blanch the bean sprouts in boiling water for 1 minute, and drain. Set aside.

Heat vegetable oil in a wok over very high heat. Set aside some spring-onion greens and red chili peppers for garnish, then stir-fry the bean sprouts with the remaining spring onions and chili peppers for about 40 seconds. Spread on a serving plate.

Reheat wok and stir-fry the chicken for 1½ minutes, until white and firm.

Pour the light soy sauce and cornstarch mixture into the wok and simmer, stirring gently, until the sauce thickens. Spread chicken on top of the bean sprouts and serve.

Stir-fried Roast Duck & Bean Sprouts

SERVES 4

½ Chinese roast duck
9 ounces bean sprouts
boiling and cold water, to
    blanch and refresh bean
    sprouts
⅔ cup chicken stock (page
    242)
1 teaspoon cornstarch
1 tablespoon light soy sauce
2 tablespoons oyster sauce

1 teaspoon granulated white
    sugar
2 tablespoons vegetable oil
1 teaspoon sesame oil
    (optional)
1 large clove garlic, thinly sliced
½ red bell pepper, cut into
    thin strips
1 fresh hot green chili pepper,
    deseeded and sliced (optional)

Leaving the skin on, debone the duck and cut the meat into slivers.

Blanch the bean sprouts in boiling water for 1 minute, then drain and refresh in cold water. Drain thoroughly.

Combine the chicken stock, cornstarch, soy and oyster sauces, and sugar. Set aside.

Heat the vegetable oil in a wok and add sesame oil (if using). Add the garlic and duck, and stir-fry for about 1 minute. Transfer to a plate. Reheat the wok and stir-fry the red bell pepper, bean sprouts and green chili pepper (if using), for about 1 minute. Return the duck to the wok and add the chicken stock and cornstarch mixture. Stir over high heat until the sauce thickens. Serve at once.

Twice-cooked Pork with Bell Pepper & Chili Pepper

SERVES 4–5

½ quantity (about 1 pound) cold simmered pork (page 185)

3 tablespoons vegetable oil

2 spring onions, sliced (white and green parts kept separate)

2 cloves garlic, finely chopped

1–4 teaspoons chili bean paste

½–1½ teaspoons granulated white sugar

1 green bell pepper, cut into 1¼-inch squares

½ red bell pepper, cut into 1¼-inch squares

1 large fresh mild red chili pepper, deseeded and thickly sliced

2 tablespoons oyster sauce

fried rice, steamed white rice or cooked noodles, to serve

Cut the pork into thin slices about 2 inches × 1 inch.

Heat the vegetable oil and stir-fry the white parts of the spring onions with the garlic, chili bean paste and sugar (to taste) for 30 seconds. Add the green and red bell peppers and red chili pepper, and stir-fry for 1½ minutes. Add the pork and continue to stir-fry until the bell peppers are almost tender and the pork is evenly coated with the sauce. Stir in the oyster sauce.

Serve at once with fried rice or steamed white rice, or over cooked noodles.

Five-spice Pork Stir-fry

SERVES 3–4

1 (14-ounce) pork fillet
1 tablespoon light soy sauce
1 teaspoon rice wine
½ teaspoon granulated white
  sugar
½ teaspoon cornstarch
⅓ cup vegetable oil
½ teaspoon Chinese five-spice
  powder
½ teaspoon ground black
  pepper or Sichuan pepper
1½ teaspoons salt
1 spring onion, finely sliced,
  for garnish

Trim the silver skin and fat from the pork fillet, and slice thinly.

Mix the light soy sauce, rice wine, sugar and cornstarch in a bowl. Add the pork slices and mix well, massaging the seasonings into the pork. Set aside to marinate for 20 minutes.

Heat half the vegetable oil in a wok over very high heat and stir-fry half the pork slices for about 1½ minutes. Transfer to a plate. Reheat the wok with the remaining vegetable oil and stir-fry the remaining pork slices.

Return all the pork to the wok and add the five-spice powder, pepper and salt. Stir-fry over very high heat until the pork slices are coated with the seasonings. Transfer to a serving dish and garnish with the spring onion.

Beef & Black Bean Stir-fry

SERVES 3–4

10½ ounces beef rump, very thinly sliced

1 tablespoon light soy sauce

2 teaspoons rice wine

¾ cup chicken stock (page 242) or water

1 teaspoon cornstarch

3 tablespoons vegetable oil

1 red bell pepper, chopped

1 green bell pepper, chopped

3 spring onions, sliced

2½ tablespoons salted (Chinese fermented) black beans, chopped

3 cloves garlic, finely chopped

1 tablespoon oyster sauce

salt (if needed)

Place the beef in a bowl and add the light soy sauce and 1 teaspoon of the rice wine. Mix well and marinate for 15 minutes. Combine the chicken stock or water and cornstarch in a small bowl and set aside.

Heat the vegetable oil in a wok over very high heat and stir-fry the red and green bell peppers and spring onions for about 1½ minutes. Transfer to a plate. Reheat the wok and add the black beans, garlic and sliced beef, and stir-fry over very high heat for about 1½ minutes, until the beef is barely cooked. Return the bell pepper and spring onions to the wok and add the oyster sauce. Pour in the chicken and cornstarch mixture stock and simmer gently until the sauce thickens. Sprinkle on the remaining rice wine and check the seasoning, adding a little salt if needed.

Stir-fried Beef with Mushrooms & Broccolini

SERVES 2–4

10½ ounces beef rump or fillet, very thinly sliced

1-inch fresh ginger

3 teaspoons rice wine

3 teaspoons soy sauce

½ teaspoon granulated white sugar

1 egg white, beaten

1 cup vegetable oil

3 tablespoons chicken stock (page 242) or water

⅓ teaspoon cornstarch

1 bunch broccolini or ⅓ head broccoli

boiling water, to cook broccolini or broccoli

4 button mushrooms, thinly sliced

1 teaspoon chopped garlic

3 spring onions (white parts only), cut into ¾-inch lengths

1½ tablespoons oyster sauce

Place the beef slices in a bowl. Drape a clean piece of cheesecloth over the bowl and grate half the ginger onto it. Squeeze the ginger juice onto the beef slices. (Discard solids.) Add half the rice wine and soy sauce to the beef slices, plus the sugar, egg white and 3 teaspoons of the vegeteble oil. Mix thoroughly. Set aside for 20 minutes to marinate.

Combine the chicken stock or water and cornstarch in a small bowl and set aside.

Finely shred the remaining ginger.

Cut the broccolini or broccoli into small florets and slice the stems. Cook in boiling water for 2 minutes. Drain and set aside.

Add the remaining vegetable oil to the wok over very high heat. When the wok is smoking hot, add the beef slices and cook for about 30 seconds, stirring with wooden chopsticks or the handle of a wooden spoon to separate the pieces. Remove the beef slices with a slotted spoon or wire skimmer and transfer to a colander to drain.

Carefully pour all but 2 tablespoons of the vegetable oil from the wok. Reheat the wok and stir-fry the mushrooms, ginger, garlic and spring onions over high heat for about 30 seconds. Add the broccolini or broccoli and stir-fry for 30 seconds.

Return the beef slices to the wok and add the oyster sauce and remaining rice wine and soy sauce. Stir-fry for about 30 seconds over high heat.

Stir the chicken stock or water and cornstarch mixture, then pour it into the wok and stir over high heat until the sauce glazes the ingredients (about 30 seconds).

✳ Broccollini is a hybrid of the cabbage family, and a cross between broccoli and Chinese kale.

Lamb & Flowering Garlic Shoots

SERVES 3–4

14 ounces lamb backstrap, very
   thinly sliced
1½ teaspoons cornstarch
2 tablespoons light soy sauce
⅓ cup chicken stock (page
   242) or water
3 tablespoons vegetable oil

1 bunch flowering garlic shoots,
   cut into 1½-inch pieces
salt
ground white pepper or
   Sichuan pepper
steamed white rice, to serve

Mix the sliced lamb with half the cornstarch and light soy sauce, and marinate for 10 minutes.

Combine the chicken stock or water and remaining cornstarch in a small bowl.

Heat half the vegetable oil in a wok over very high heat and stir-fry half the lamb slices for about 40 seconds. Transfer to a plate. Add the remaining vegetable oil to the wok and stir-fry the remaining lamb slices for 40 seconds. Set aside with the first batch of lamb slices.

Stir-fry the garlic shoots for 1 minute.

Pour the chicken stock or water and cornstarch mixture into the wok and stir over high heat until the sauce thickens. Add the remaining light soy sauce and return the lamb slices to the wok. Cook for about 20 seconds, stirring gently. Season to taste with salt and ground white or Sichuan pepper. Serve at once with steamed white rice.

✻ Lamb backstrap is the of eye short loin. Substitute lamb rib chops; you may need more per serving. Chinese chives can be substituted for garlic shoots.

Stir-fried Lamb & Bell Pepper

SERVES 3–4

10½ ounces lamb backstrap
  (eye of short loin), very
  thinly sliced
1½ tablespoons light soy sauce
1 teaspoon sesame oil
1½ tablespoons oyster sauce
½ teaspoon granulated white
  sugar
2 teaspoons rice wine
½ cup chicken stock (page 242)
  or water
1 teaspoon cornstarch

3 tablespoons vegetable oil
½ red bell pepper, thinly sliced
½ green bell pepper, thinly
  sliced
½ yellow bell pepper, thinly
  sliced
1 large fresh hot red chili
  pepper, deseeded and sliced
2 cloves garlic, finely chopped
2 thin slices fresh ginger, finely
  shredded
1 spring onion, finely sliced

Place the lamb slices in a bowl and add 2 teaspoons light soy sauce and the sesame oil. Mix well and set aside to marinate for 20 minutes.

In another bowl combine the remaining light soy sauce, the oyster sauce, sugar, rice wine, chicken stock or water and cornstarch. Mix well and set aside.

Heat the vegetable oil in a wok over high heat and stir-fry the bell peppers, red chili pepper, garlic, ginger and spring onion for 1 minute. Transfer to a plate.

Reheat the wok and stir-fry the lamb slices, in two batches, for about 1 minute. Return the cooked bell pepper mixture to the wok and stir-fry over high heat to combine.

Pour the light soy sauce mixrture into the wok and stir over high heat until the sauce glazes the ingredients (about 30 seconds). Serve at once.

Fish with Black Beans, Chili Pepper & Garlic Sauce

SERVES 4

1 pound 2 ounces firm white
   fish (such as cod, sea bass,
   monkfish)
2 ½ teaspoons cornstarch
salt
¾ teaspoon granulated white
   sugar
2 ½ tablespoons salted (Chinese
   fermented) black beans
1 tablespoon light soy sauce

1 tablespoon sesame oil
1 large fresh hot red chili
   pepper, deseeded and
   chopped
3 cloves garlic, finely chopped
3 teaspoons rice wine
water, to mix with cornstarch
3 tablespoons vegetable oil
white rice and green vegetables
   to serve

Cut the fish into ⅜-inch slices. Place in a bowl, add about 2 teaspoons of the cornstarch and ½ teaspoon salt and mix well. Marinate for 20 minutes.

Add the sugar to the salted black beans and lightly crush or chop the beans. Add the light soy sauce, sesame oil, red chili pepper, garlic and rice wine, and mix well.

In another bowl combine the remaining ½ teaspoon cornstarch with ⅓ cup water, and set aside. >

Heat the vegetable oil in a wok over high heat. When almost smoking hot, add the black bean mixture and fry for 30 seconds, stirring. Add the fish and cook on medium heat, turning gently, for 1½–2 minutes.

Stir the cornstarch and water mixture, then pour it into the wok. Simmer, stirring, until the sauce thickens and becomes translucent. Continue to cook gently until the fish is tender. Check for seasoning, adding salt to taste.

Serve with steamed white rice and a green vegetable.

Prawn Stir-fry with Garlic Chives & Chili Oil

SERVES 4

24 medium-sized raw (green) prawns, butterflied but tails left on
salt
1½ teaspoons cornstarch
½ egg white, well beaten
water, to mix with cornstarch
2½ tablespoons vegetable oil
½ bunch garlic chives, cut into 1½-inch lengths
1–3 teaspoons chili oil (optional)
steamed white rice and green vegetable, to serve

Place the prawns in a bowl and add ½ teaspoon salt, 1 teaspoon of the cornstarch and the egg white. Mix well and marinate for 20 minutes.

Mix the remaining cornstarch with ⅓ cup water and set aside.

Heat the vegetable oil in a wok and stir-fry the garlic chives over high heat for about 20 seconds. Transfer to a plate.

Reheat the wok and stir-fry the prawns until firm and opaque.

Return the garlic chives to the wok and fry briefly. For a spicy prawn stir-fry, add chili oil to taste. Stir the cornstarch-water mixture, then pour it into the wok and simmer, stirring occasionally, on low–medium heat until the sauce thickens. Check for seasoning, adding salt if needed.

Serve with steamed white rice and a green vegetable.

Prawn & Asparagus Stir-fry

SERVES 4

24 medium-sized raw (green) prawns, butterflied but tails left on
1½-inch piece fresh ginger
2 teaspoons rice wine
salt and ground white pepper
1 bunch asparagus
boiling water, to blanch asparagus
2½ tablespoons vegetable oil
2 spring onions, cut into ¾-inch lengths
steamed white rice or rice noodles, to serve

Place the prawns in a bowl. Drape a clean piece of cheesecloth over the bowl and grate the ginger onto it. Squeeze the ginger juice into the bowl, then add the rice wine and a large pinch each of salt and ground white pepper, and mix. Marinate the prawns for 15 minutes, stirring several times.

Cut thick asparagus spears on a diagonal into long thin slices, or cut thin asparagus spears into 2¼-inch lengths. Blanch the asparagus in boiling water for 30 seconds, and drain.

Heat the vegetable oil in a wok until almost smoking, then stir-fry the asparagus for about 30 seconds. Transfer to a plate.

Stir-fry the prawns and spring onions for 1 minute, or until the prawns are firm and pink. Return the asparagus to the wok and add any ginger marinade from the bowl. Toss over high heat for a few seconds. Serve over steamed white rice or rice noodles.

Stir-fried Squid with Snow Peas & Bell Pepper

You yu bao

SERVES 3–5

14 ounces fresh squid or
   cuttlefish tubes
12 snow peas
boiling water and cold water, to
   blanch and refresh snow peas
$2/3$ teaspoon cornstarch
water, to mix with cornstarch
1 cup vegetable oil
1 large clove garlic, finely
   chopped

1 red bell pepper, cut into
   $3/4$-inch squares
1 small onion, 'Asian cut' (see
   page 10)
1 spring onion, sliced on a
   diagonal
1 tablespoon rice wine
1 tablespoon light soy sauce
salt and ground white pepper
steamed white rice, to serve

Cut each squid along one side and open out. Using a sharp knife, score the inner surface in a cross-hatch pattern, then cut into 1½-inches × ¾-inch pieces.

Blanch the snow peas in boiling water, and refresh in cold water. Drain.

In a small bowl mix the cornstarch with ⅓ cup water, and set aside.

Heat the vegetable oil in a wok to 350°F. Fry the squid for about 30 seconds. Remove using a slotted spoon or wire skimmer and transfer to a plate. Carefully pour off the vegetable oil into a bowl and reserve.

Reheat the wok (without adding any oil) and when almost smoking hot, cook the garlic for 10 seconds. Return the squid to the wok and cook for about 20 seconds. Transfer the squid and garlic to a plate.

Add 2 tablespoons of the frying oil to the wok and heat over high heat. Stir-fry the bell pepper and onion for about 1 minute, until softened. Add the spring onion and stir-fry briefly, then add the snow peas and return the squid and garlic to the wok. Stir-fry for 20 seconds, then pour in the rice wine and light soy sauce, and add a pinch each of salt and ground white pepper.

Pour the cornstarch and water mixture into the wok and simmer, stirring, until the sauce thickens and glazes the ingredients (about 30 seconds).

Serve at once with steamed white rice.

✳ Butterflied prawns could replace the squid.

Noodles & Rice

Steamed white rice is served with almost every Chinese meal. The easiest way to prepare it is in a rice cooker— you'll get perfect rice every time and have more time to concentrate on other tasks. (If you don't have a rice cooker, there's a recipe for steamed white rice on page 239.) Medium-grain white rice is the best choice.

Fried rice can be served as a meal or side dish. Sticky or glutinous rice, with its chewy texture, is an alternative you might enjoy from time to time. Rice is also used to make the famous breakfast soup 'congee', or 'xi fan' as its simplest version is called.

Noodles make a quick and easy meal. Egg noodles are like thin spaghetti, and they can be teamed with almost any seasoning or ingredient. Rice noodles are more delicate and are generally paired with milder seasonings — they are delicious in soups.

‹ CONGEE (RICE BREAKFAST SOUP) (PAGE 108)

Congee (Rice Breakfast Soup)
Xi fan

SERVES 4–6

1 cup medium-grain white rice

2 tablespoons vegetable oil

salt

water, to boil rice

7–10½ ounces thinly sliced raw fish, chicken, rump steak or prawns

lightly salted boiling water, to blanch beef, poultry or seafood

3 spring onions, finely chopped

4 thin slices fresh ginger, finely shredded

3 tablespoons light soy sauce

3 teaspoons sesame oil

2–3 tablespoons finely chopped fresh cilantro

4–6 eggs (optional)

Mix the rice and vegetable oil with 2¼ quarts water in a saucepan and bring to a boil. Reduce heat and simmer, partially covered, for about 1½ hours, until creamy.

Blanch the beef, poultry or seafood in lightly salted boiling water, and drain immediately. Arrange on a platter with the spring onions.

Mix the ginger with the light soy sauce and sesame oil in a small serving bowl. Place the cilantro in another small serving bowl.

At the table, diners add a selection of ingredients to their bowl of hot congee. If using eggs, diners should crack an egg into their bowl while the soup is still very hot, so the egg is partially cooked.

Grilled Rice Cakes with Chinese Greens & Oyster Sauce

SERVES 2–3

9 ounces fresh rice sheets (wide strips of shahe fen, or rice noodles)
2 tablespoons peanut oil
2–3 teaspoons sesame oil
1 bunch Chinese water spinach (baby spinach, kale or watercress), tough stems removed

1 clove garlic, finely chopped
water to steam spinach or other greens
2 tablespoons oyster sauce
1 tablespoon light soy sauce
1 spring onion, finely sliced, for garnish

Take the rice sheets out of the package and, without unfolding the sheets, cut into 2-inch blocks.

Combine the peanut oil and sesame oil, and brush some over the noodle blocks. Pour the remaining oil into a wok over high heat. Sear the noodle blocks on all sides, then transfer to a serving platter and keep warm.

Add the water spinach or the greens and garlic to the wok, and stir-fry for 1 minute. Add 2 tablespoons water, cover the wok and steam for 1 minute. Uncover and continue to cook over high heat, adding the oyster and light soy sauces. Mix well.

Surround the rice cakes with the cooked greens and spoon over the liquid from the wok. Garnish with spring onion and serve.

Steamed Rice Sheets with Prawns
Fen bau zheng

SERVES 2–4

4 pieces fresh rice sheet, each
   8 inches × 5 inches)
hot water, to soften rice sheets
32 medium-sized raw (green)
   prawns, shelled and deveined
2 thin slices fresh ginger, finely
   shredded

3 tablespoons light soy sauce
1 teaspoon Chinese black
   vinegar (or balsamic)
½ teaspoon chili oil or
   1 teaspoon sesame oil

Place the rice sheets in a bowl of hot water to soften. Leave for 20–30 seconds only, then remove and spread on a clean kitchen towel.

Combine the prawns and ginger, then divide among the rice sheets, arranging them in the center across the shortest side. Roll up each rice sheet to enclose the filling.

Place the prawn rolls on a plate and put into a steamer. Gently steam for 8–9 minutes.

Combine the light soy sauce, black vinegar and chili or sesame oil, and pour over the rolls.

Serve at once.

✳ You can replace the prawns with 8 ounces red roast pork (page 179). Finely dice the pork and combine it with 2 finely chopped spring onions (instead of the ginger).

Fried Rice
Chao fan

1 quantity steamed white rice
(page 239)

2½ tablespoons vegetable oil

2 eggs

salt

2 slices bacon, diced

3 ounces small shelled raw
(green) prawns, deveined

3 ounces red roast pork (page
179), roast chicken
or ham, diced

½ cup cooked green peas

3 spring onions, finely
chopped (reserve some
greens for garnish)

1 teaspoon sesame oil

salt and ground white pepper

2–4 teaspoons light soy sauce

If possible, cook the rice a few hours ahead so it can dry out a little; otherwise spread hot cooked rice on a large plate to cool.

Heat a wok and add 1 teaspoon of the vegetable oil. Swirl the wok so that most of the inside surface is oiled, then beat the eggs with a pinch of salt and pour into the hot wok. Again swirl the wok, this time to spread the egg into a thin crêpe. Carefully slide the crêpe from the wok onto a plate.

Reheat the wok and sauté the bacon until crisp. Add a little extra vegetable oil to the wok and stir-fry the prawns and meat or poultry for about 30 seconds, until the prawns are firm. Add the peas and spring onion (reserving some spring-onion greens for garnish) and mix well.

Add the remaining vegetable oil and the sesame oil to the wok, along with the rice. Stir-fry over high heat until the rice is glossy, hot and well mixed with the other ingredients. Season to taste with salt, ground white pepper and light soy sauce.

Chop up the egg and fold through the rice. Garnish with spring-onion greens. Serve hot.

Fried Rice Wrapped in an Omelette

SERVES 2

3 eggs
1 teaspoon light soy sauce
1 spring onion, finely chopped
salt and ground white pepper
1½ tablespoons vegetable oil

2 cups fried rice (page 112)
2 tablespoons oyster sauce, to
  serve

Whisk the eggs with the light soy sauce, spring onion and a pinch each of salt and ground white pepper.

Heat 1¼ tablespoons vegetable oil in a wok and stir-fry the fried rice until well heated. Transfer to a plate.

Wipe out the wok and heat the remaining teaspoon of vegetable oil. Pour in half the eggs and swirl to spread into a thin omelette. Lift the sides of the omelette so the uncooked eggs can run underneath, and when almost cooked and golden brown on the underside, flip and briefly cook the other side. Slide the omelette onto a plate and keep warm. Cook the remaining eggs in the same way.

Place the omelettes on two plates and add half the rice to each. Wrap the rice inside the omelette and serve at once, drizzled with oyster sauce.

✳ This makes a delicious light meal for two using leftover fried rice.

Clay-pot Chicken Rice
Jing ji farn

SERVES 4–6

14 ounces chicken thigh fillets,
cut into ¾-inch cubes

2 tablespoons light soy sauce

3 teaspoons rice wine

3 spring onions

2 cups medium-grain white rice

4 thin slices fresh ginger, finely
shredded

2½ tablespoons dried shrimp,
soaked in hot water for
25 minutes

8 button mushrooms or dried
shiitake mushrooms (soak
dried mushrooms in hot
water for 25 minutes)

2–3 cups chicken stock (page
242)

2 tablespoons vegetable oil

1–2 dried Chinese sausages,
sliced (optional)

salt and ground white pepper

Combine the chicken with the light soy sauce and rice wine and marinate for
10 minutes.

Cut the white parts and half the greens of the spring onions into ¾-inch lengths.
Finely chop the remaining greens and set aside.

Spread the rice evenly in a clay pot and add the ginger and white and green
spring-onion pieces.

Strain the liquid from the shrimp and mushrooms into a saucepan and add enough chicken stock to make up to 3½ cups. Bring to a boil and add the chicken, mushrooms and dried shrimp, then reduce heat and simmer for 10 minutes.

Strain the liquid over the rice, add the vegetable oil and cover. Cook on medium heat until the liquid is level with the rice.

Spread the shrimp, mushrooms, chicken, sliced sausage (if using) and some of the chopped spring-onion greens over the rice. Cover tightly and cook for 10–12 minutes, until the chicken is tender and the rice cooked.

Stir well and check for seasoning, adding salt and ground white pepper to taste.

Garnish with the remaining spring-onion greens and serve in the pot.

✳ Chinese sausage is a dark and thin pork sausage that loosk like pepperoni, but is sweeter. Substitute with chorizo, salami or diced ham.

Sticky Rice & Chinese Sausage

SERVES 4

2¼ cups long-grain glutinous (sticky or sweet) rice

water, to soak rice

2½ fluid ounces vegetable or peanut oil

simmering water, to steam rice

5 dried shiitake mushrooms, soaked in hot water for 25 minutes

2 tablespoons dried shrimp, soaked in hot water for 25 minutes

3 spring onions, chopped

2 Chinese sausages (or chorizo, salami, or ham), finely sliced

5–6 sprigs cilantro, coarsely chopped

salt

2 tablespoons light soy sauce

Cover the rice with water and soak overnight (or for at least 3 hours).

Drain the rice and place in a steamer lined with a clean piece of cheesecloth. Drizzle on 1½ tablespoons of the vegetable or peanut oil and stir through. Place over simmering water, cover, and steam for about 35 minutes, until cooked.

Drain the mushrooms, trim the tough stems and finely slice the mushroom caps. Drain the dried shrimp.

Heat the remaining vegetable or peanut oil in a wok over high heat and stir-fry the spring onions briefly. Add the mushrooms, shrimp and sausages, and stir-fry for 1 minute. Add the rice and toss over high heat until well mixed, then add the cilantro, a few pinches of salt and the light soy sauce.

Flat Rice Noodles with Lamb & Broccoli in Oyster Sauce

SERVES 3–4

9 ounces lamb backstrap or
 fillet, thinly sliced

1 tablespoon light soy sauce

2 teaspoons dark soy sauce

2 teaspoons rice wine

1½ teaspoons cornstarch

1 clove garlic, crushed

1 pound 2 ounces fresh rice
 sheets

½ cup chicken stock (page 242)

7 ounces broccoli or
 broccolini, cut into small
 pieces

lightly salted boiling water, to
 parboil broccoli or broccolini

3 tablespoons vegetable oil

2 teaspoons sesame oil
 (optional)

2 spring onions, cut into
 ¾-inch lengths

6 oyster or button mushrooms,
 thickly sliced

3 tablespoons oyster sauce

ground white pepper

In a bowl, combine the sliced lamb with the soy sauces, rice wine, half the cornstarch and the garlic. Mix well and set aside to marinate for 20 minutes.

Cut the fresh rice sheets into ribbon noodles about ⅝-inch wide. Place in a colander and rinse with warm water. Let drain.

Stir the remaining cornstarch into the chicken stock and set aside.

Parboil the broccoli or broccolini in lightly salted boiling water for about 1½ minutes, and drain.

Heat the vegetable oil in a wok and when almost smoking add the sesame oil (if using). Fry the rice noodles lightly, and spread on a serving platter.

Stir-fry the lamb slices for 1 minute, and transfer to a plate. Add the broccoli or broccolini to the wok, along with the spring onions and mushrooms, and stir-fry for 1 minute. Add the chicken stock and cornstarch mixture and half the oyster sauce, and simmer, stirring often, until the sauce thickens. Return the lamb slices to the wok and stir to coat with the sauce.

Spread the lamb slices and vegetables over the noodles, season generously with ground white pepper and drizzle on the remaining oyster sauce. Serve at once.

Egg Noodles with Chicken & Crab Meat Sauce

Dan mian ji

SERVES 2–3

½ pound flat dried egg noodles

lightly salted water, to boil egg noodles

7 ounces chicken breast fillet, coarsely minced

1 teaspoon rice wine

1²/₃ teaspoons cornstarch

1¹/₃ cups chicken stock (page 242)

¾ cup vegetable oil

2 teaspoons sesame oil (optional)

3 spring onions, finely sliced (white and green parts kept separate)

5 ounces cooked crab meat

3 teaspoons light soy sauce

salt and ground white pepper

3 egg whites, well beaten

Boil the egg noodles in lightly salted water for 6–7 minutes, until tender. Drain and divide among serving bowls.

Combine the chicken with the rice wine and ½ teaspoon of the cornstarch.

Stir the remaining cornstarch into the chicken stock and set aside.

Heat the vegetable oil in a wok and stir-fry the chicken over very high heat, stirring to break up any lumps, until the chicken is white. ➤

Place a strainer over a bowl and pour in the chicken and vegetable oil. Drain well.

Return 2 tablespoons of the vegetable oil to the wok and add the sesame oil (if using). Over medium–high heat, stir-fry the spring-onion whites, crab meat and light soy sauce for 30 seconds, stirring continuously. Return the chicken to the wok and pour in the chicken stock and cornstarch mixture. Simmer, stirring, until the sauce thickens. Season to taste with salt and ground white pepper, then remove from the heat. Slowly drizzle in the egg whites and do not stir until they set in fine white strands in the sauce.

Reheat the sauce briefly, then pour it over the noodles. Garnish with the spring-onion greens, and serve at once.

Noodles with Spicy Pork & Tofu

SERVES 3–4

10½ ounces dried egg noodles
lightly salted boiling water, to
   cook egg noodles
3½ ounces minced pork
1 teaspoon rice wine
1 teaspoon dark soy sauce
2 tablespoons vegetable oil
¼ cup finely chopped salt-
   pickled vegetables
⅓ cup finely diced firm tofu

1 Chinese sausage (chorizo,
   salami, or ham), finely diced
2 spring onions, finely
   chopped
2–4 teaspoons chili bean paste
2 tablespoons light soy sauce
water, to add to pork mixture
Sichuan pepper, to serve
chili oil or Chinese black
   vinegar, to serve

Cook the egg noodles in lightly salted boiling water for about 6 minutes, or until barely tender. Drain, and divide among 3–4 bowls.

Season the pork with the rice wine and dark soy sauce.

Heat the vegetable oil in a wok until almost smoking and stir-fry the pork with the salt-pickled vegetables, tofu, sausage, spring onions and chili bean paste for about 2½ minutes, until the pork is well cooked. Add the light soy sauce and 1 cup water and bring to a boil.

Divide the pork mixture evenly among the bowls.

Serve at once with Sichuan pepper and chili oil or Chinese black vinegar.

Sichuan Bean-thread Noodles with Cabbage & Bean Sprouts

SERVES 3–4

5 ounces bean-thread
  vermicelli
boiling water, to soak vermicelli
2 tablespoons dried shrimp,
  soaked in hot water for
  25 minutes
8 small dried shiitake
  mushrooms, soaked in hot
  water for 25 minutes
2 tablespoons vegetable oil
2 teaspoons sesame oil

1 large onion, finely sliced
5 ounces bean sprouts
3 cups finely shredded cabbage
1–2 fresh hot red chili peppers,
  deseeded and chopped
2 tablespoons light soy sauce
1–3 teaspoons chili oil
1–1½ teaspoons sugar
chopped fresh cilantro, for
  garnish

Soak the bean thread vermicelli in boiling water for 4–5 minutes, until tender. Drain. Strain the shrimp and mushrooms. Trim the tough stems from the mushrooms and finely chop or slice the mushroom caps.

Heat the vegetable oil in a wok and when almost smoking add the sesame oil and onion. Stir-fry for 1 minute, until lightly cooked. Add the shrimp and mushrooms, bean sprouts, cabbage and red chili peppers, and stir-fry for about 2 minutes, until the cabbage and onion are soft. Add the light soy sauce and bean-thread vermicelli, and mix well. Season to taste with chili oil and sugar, and mix well.

Garnish with the cilantro to serve.

Fresh Rice Noodles with Meat, Seafood & Vegetables

SERVES 2–3

²/₃ cup chicken stock (page 242)

²/₃ teaspoon cornstarch

14 ounces fresh rice noodles

boiling water, to pour over rice noodles

2 teaspoons sesame oil

3½ ounces chicken breast, thinly sliced

3½ ounces pork fillet, thinly sliced

12 medium-sized raw (green) prawns, shelled and deveined

2 teaspoons light soy sauce

1 teaspoon rice wine

salt and ground white pepper

¹/₃ cup vegetable oil

1 small carrot, thinly sliced on a diagonal

1 celery stalk, thinly sliced on a diagonal

3 baby bok choy, cut in half lengthwise

water, to steam vegetables

½ cup sliced oyster mushrooms

2 spring onions, chopped (white and green parts kept separate)

1 thin slice fresh ginger, finely shredded

2 tablespoons oyster sauce

Mix the chicken stock and cornstarch in a small bowl and set aside.

Place the rice noodles in a colander, pour boiling water over and gently separate using chopsticks. Drain, then toss the sesame oil through the noodles to prevent them from sticking. **>**

Combine the chicken, pork and prawns in a bowl and season with the light soy sauce, rice wine and a pinch each of salt and ground white pepper. Set aside.

Heat 2 tablespoons of the vegetable oil in a wok on very high heat and stir-fry the carrot, celery and bok choy for 40 seconds. Add 2 tablespoons water, cover and steam for 1 minute. Remove the lid, add the oyster mushrooms and spring-onion whites, and toss until the liquid evaporates. Transfer to a plate.

Reheat the wok with the remaining vegetable oil and stir-fry the chicken, pork, prawns and ginger, for about 1½ minutes on very high heat. Return the vegetables to the wok, add the oyster sauce and rice noodles, and stir gently to combine. Cook for about 1½ minutes, until the rice noodles are heated through.

Garnish with spring-onion greens and serve at once.

Duck Noodles in Soy–Ginger Sauce

Ya lei mian

SERVES 4

2 teaspoons sesame oil

2 tablespoons vegetable oil

½ duck (about 1 pound
9 ounces), chopped into
2-inch pieces

3 tablespoons dark soy sauce

3 tablespoons rice wine

1½-inch piece fresh ginger,
roughly chopped

2 star anise

⅓ teaspoon Sichuan
peppercorns (optional)

water, to cover duck

1 pound 2 ounces fresh udon
noodles

boiling water, to cover noodles
and blanch vegetables

1 bunch baby bok choy or
Chinese mustard greens, cut
in half

Heat the sesame and vegetable oils in a wok and fry the duck, in batches, until well browned.

Place the duck in a saucepan with the dark soy sauce, rice wine, ginger and spices. Add enough water to barely cover the duck, then bring to a boil. Reduce heat and simmer for about 45 minutes, until the duck is tender.

Pour boiling water over the udon noodles and gently separate. Drain.

Blanch the vegetables in lightly salted boiling water for 2 minutes. Drain.

Carefully pour the sesame and vegetable oil from the wok. Reheat the wok and stir-fry the vegetables and noodles for 1 minute, then serve into bowls. Use tongs to transfer the cooked duck to each bowl, then strain some of the sauce over.

Seafood

China has a long coastline and many large rivers, so fish and seafood have always been important in regional Chinese cooking. A wide range of fish and shellfish is used, including a number of exotic fresh and dried varieties like bêche de mer (sea cucumber), jellyfish and fresh-water turtles, which are rarely eaten elsewhere in the world.

Ocean and freshwater fish and prawns are popular for everyday meals. They are cooked without fuss and may be simply flavored with salty seasonings like oyster sauce and fish sauce, spiced with Sichuan pepper or chili bean paste, or teamed with classic flavors like ginger and onions.

Chinese cooks create spectacular dishes with inexpensive mussels and clams, squid and cuttlefish, and banquet fare with crabs and fish cooked whole. Seafood stir-fries can be found in the stir-fries section (pages 98–105).

< FISH & TOFU CLAY POT (PAGE 134)

Fish & Tofu Clay Pot

SERVES 4

14 ounces catfish, cod or tilapia, cut into 1½-inch cubes

½ teaspoon salt

2 cups vegetable oil

8–10 cubes deep-fried tofu puffs

boiling water, to cover tofu puffs

½ cup cornstarch, plus extra for thickening (optional)

2 teaspoons sesame oil

6 ounces Chinese cabbage (wombok), roughly chopped

8–10 small fresh shiitake or button mushrooms, quartered

2 tablespoons dark soy sauce

1½ tablespoons light soy sauce

1 tablespoon rice wine

1½ teaspoons grated ginger

¼ cup chopped spring onions

boiling water, to combine sauce and cold water, to thicken cornstarch

1–2 tablespoons chopped cilantro (optional), for garnish

steamed white rice, to serve

Place the fish in a bowl, add the salt and set aside for a few minutes.

Heat the vegetable oil in a wok to 350°F. Fry the tofu puffs briefly, until golden. Use a slotted spoon to remove and transfer to a bowl. Cover the tofu puffs with boiling water and steep for 1 minute, then drain. Set aside.

Coat the fish lightly with cornstarch, shaking off excess.

Reheat the vegetable oil and fry the fish, stirring slowly to keep the fish from sticking together, until lightly golden (about 1 minute). Remove with a slotted spoon and set aside on paper towels to drain.

Carefully pour all but 1 tablespoon vegetable oil from the wok. Add the sesame oil and stir-fry the cabbage and mushrooms for about 1 minute. Remove wok from the heat.

Combine the soy sauces, rice wine, ginger and half the spring onions in a clay pot and add 1½ cups boiling water. Simmer, uncovered, for 2 minutes. Add the fish, Chinese cabbage, mushrooms and tofu puffs, and simmer, covered, for about 5 minutes.

If desired, the dark and light sauce can be thickened with 1½–2 teaspoons cornstarch mixed with 3 tablespoons cold water: pour the cornstarch mixture into the sauce and simmer gently, stirring from time to time, until thickened.

Scatter with the remaining spring onions and the chopped cilantro (if using). Serve at once with steamed white rice.

Steamed Whole Fish with Ginger & Spring Onions
Qing zheng yu

SERVES 2–3

1 whole fresh snapper or
    orange roughy (about 1
    pound 14 ounces)
boiling water, to steam fish
3 thin slices fresh ginger, finely
    shredded
2 spring onions, finely
    shredded

1 tablespoon rice wine
2 tablespoons light soy sauce
2 tablespoons vegetable oil
2–3 sprigs cilantro, for garnish

Rinse and dry the fish, then make several deep cuts across each side. Bring water to a boil in the base of a steamer.

Place the fish on a steamer basket and scatter evenly with the ginger and spring onions. Combine the rice wine, light soy sauce and vegetable oil, and pour it over the fish.

Place the steamer basket in the steamer, cover, and steam the fish for 15 minutes, or until the flesh is tender and cooked through.

Garnish with cilantro sprigs and serve.

Pepper–Salt Fish on Crisp-fried Greens

SERVES 4

1 pound 2 ounces thick firm white fish fillets (such as grouper, orange roughy, mahi mahi, or snapper), cut into 1¼-inch × 2-inch strips
2 teaspoons rice wine
1 teaspoon crushed ginger
pinch of salt
pinch of granulated white sugar
1½ cups all-purpose flour
¼-ounce packet dry yeast
water, to mix with yeast
vegetable oil for deep-frying
1 large bunch bok choy, leafy tops coarsely shredded (stems discarded)
2–3 teaspoons Sichuan pepper–salt (page 240) or sweet and sour sauce (page 236), to serve

Place the fish in a bowl and season with the rice wine, ginger, salt and sugar. Mix well and marinate for 2 hours, turning from time to time.

Sift flour into a bowl. Add yeast and about 1 cup water and stir to make a smooth batter. Cover the bowl and leave for 40 minutes.

Heat the vegetable oil in a wok to 375°F, then reduce heat slightly. Dip fish pieces, one by one, into the batter, coating generously. Carefully lower the fish pieces into the vegetable oil, in batches, and stir with wooden chopsticks or a slotted spoon to prevent sticking. Increase the heat and fry until golden brown and puffy (about 1 minute), then remove with a wire skimmer and place on a rack set over paper towesl to drain.

When all the fish is cooked, reheat the oil to 350°F and fry the shredded bok choy leaves until crisp and crackling (45–60 seconds). Remove and drain well on paper towels.

Arrange fish and crisp bok choy leaves on a serving plate. Sprinkle with pepper–salt, or serve with bowls of sweet and sour sauce for dipping.

Sichuan Fish in Chili-bean Sauce

Si chuan dou ban jiang yu

SERVES 4

1 pound 2 ounces snapper,
  catfish or perch fillets, cut
  into ⅝-inch slices
1½ tablespoons rice wine
½ teaspoon salt
1 tablespoon cornstarch
1½ cups peanut oil
⅝-inch piece fresh ginger,
  grated
3 cloves garlic, finely chopped
2 spring onions, chopped
  (white and green parts kept
  separate)

3 tablespoons chili bean paste
1 teaspoon granulated white
  sugar
water, to prepare sauce and
  cold water, to thicken
½–¾ teaspoon Chinese black
  vinegar or balsamic vinegar
steamed rice and green
  vegetable, to serve

Place the fish in a bowl and add the rice wine, salt and 2 teaspoons of the corn-starch. Mix well. Set aside for 10 minutes.

Heat the peanut oil in a wok over high heat. Once almost smoking, add half the fish and fry until lightly browned (about 1 minute), then transfer to a plate using a slotted spoon or wire skimmer. Cook the remaining fish.

Carefully pour all but 2 tablespoons peanut oil from the wok. Reheat the wok and add the ginger, garlic, spring-onion whites, chili bean paste and sugar. Stir over high heat for 1 minute. Pour in 1½ cups water and bring back to a boil. Return the fish to the wok and simmer for about 10 minutes, basting frequently with the spicy sauce.

Stir the remaining cornstarch into 2 tablespoons cold water and pour into the wok. Simmer until the sauce thickens, then add the spring-onion greens and vinegar to taste, and check for salt.

Serve at once, with steamed white rice and a green vegetable.

Seafood over Sizzling Rice Cakes

SERVES 4-6

2 ½ tablespoons vegetable oil
⅓ cup diced celery
⅓ cup diced spring onions
2 teaspoons finely chopped
   fresh ginger
5 ounces squid, diced
8–10 raw (green) prawns,
   shelled and deveined, sliced
5 ounces firm fish fillets (such
   as grouper, orange roughy,
   mahi mahi, or snapper),
   diced
5 ounces shelled clams or
   mussels

¾ cup thinly sliced button
   mushrooms
¼ cup diced bamboo shoots
2 ½ cups chicken stock (page
   242) or fish stock (page 243)
2 teaspoons rice wine
2 tablespoons dark soy sauce
1–3 teaspoons chili oil
1 tablespoon cornstarch
water, to mix with cornstarch
salt and ground white pepper
vegetable oil, for deep-frying
8–12 crisp rice cakes

Heat the vegetable oil in a wok over high heat. Stir-fry the celery, spring onions and ginger for 30 seconds. Add the seafood, mushrooms and bamboo shoots, and stir-fry briefly.

Pour in the chicken stock, rice wine, dark soy sauce and chili oil, and bring to a boil. >

Stir the cornstarch into about 3 tablespoons water, and stir it into the sauce. Simmer, stirring, until the sauce thickens and becomes translucent. Continue to simmer gently for 5–6 minutes, then season to taste with salt and ground white pepper.

While the seafood is cooking, heat the vegetable oil for deep-frying to 350°F. Add the rice cakes and fry until golden brown. Divide rice cakes among individual serving bowls.

As soon as the seafood is cooked, arrange it over the rice cakes. Serve at once.

✳ Crisp rice cakes are blocks of puffy dried rice. They are often deep-fried or baked and served sizzling hot with a thick soup. They are sold in packages in Asian food stores.

Garlic & Black Bean Mussels

SERVES 4–5

1 cup fish stock (page 243) or
 water
1 ¼ teaspoons cornstarch
1 ½ tablespoons oyster sauce
⅓ cup vegetable oil
1 tablespoon salted (Chinese
 fermented) black beans,
 chopped
1 tablespoon chopped garlic
1 thin slice fresh ginger,
 chopped
1 fresh hot red chili pepper,

deseeded and chopped
¼ red bell pepper, diced
¼ green bell pepper, diced
1 small onion, diced
1 pound 2 ounces shelled
 mussels
1 ½ teaspoons sesame oil
salt and ground white pepper
pinch of granulated white sugar
 (if needed)
steamed white rice, to serve

Combine the fish stock or water, cornstarch and oyster sauce in a bowl. Set aside.

Heat the vegetable oil in a wok over high heat. Add the salted black beans, garlic, ginger and red chili pepper, and stir-fry for 20 seconds. Add the bell peppers and onion, and stir-fry for 40 seconds. Add the mussels and stir-fry for 30 seconds.

Pour the fish stock or water and cornstarch mixture into the wok and simmer, stirring, until the sauce thickens and becomes translucent (about 1 ½ minutes). Pour in the sesame oil. Add salt and ground white pepper to taste, and a pinch of sugar if needed.

Serve with steamed white rice.

Calamari & Black Mushroom Clay Pot

You ru gu sar po

SERVES 4

8 dried shiitake mushrooms, soaked in 1½ cups hot water for 25 minutes

1 pound 2 ounces small or large squid or cuttlefish tubes

2 tablespoons vegetable oil

4 spring onions, cut into 1¼-inch pieces

2 cloves garlic, chopped

3–4 thin slices fresh ginger

2 tablespoons light soy sauce

2 teaspoons dark soy sauce

2 teaspoons rice wine

½ teaspoon lightly crushed Sichuan peppercorns

1½ ounces bean-thread vermicelli, softened in hot water and drained

½ medium-sized carrot, sliced

1½ ounces sliced bamboo shoots or water chestnuts

1⅓ teaspoons cornstarch

cold water, to prepare sauce

salt or sugar (if needed)

1 tablespoone oyster sauce

2 tablespoons chopped fresh cilantro

Drain the mushrooms, reserving the liquid. Trim the tough stems and cut the mushroom caps in half. Set aside.

Clean small squid and leave whole. Score the underside of large squid and cut into 1½-inch pieces. ❯

Heat the vegetable oil in a clay pot and sauté the spring onions, garlic and ginger. Add the mushrooms, squid, light and dark soy sauces, rice wine and pepper-corns, and pour in the mushroom soaking liquid. Cover and simmer gently for 20 minutes. Add the bean-thread vermicelli, carrot and bamboo shoots or water chestnuts, and simmer an additional 10 minutes.

Stir the cornstarch into 3 tablespoons cold water and pour into the pot. Stir slowly over medium heat until the sauce thickens. Check for seasoning, adding a little salt if needed – or if too salty, add a few pinches of sugar. Stir in the oyster sauce and cilantro.

Serve immediately, in the clay pot.

Scallops on the Shell with Garlic & Chili Pepper

Xian bai la jiao suan

SERVES 4–6

24 scallops on the half shell
8 very thin slices fresh ginger
1 large fresh mild red chili pepper, deseeded and very finely chopped
1 clove garlic, very finely chopped
1 tablespoon light soy sauce

1 teaspoon sesame oil
2 teaspoons light corn oil
water, to steam scallops
1 tablespoon rice wine
1 small bunch fresh cilantro (reserve some small leaves for garnish)

Run the blade of a knife beneath each scallop to loosen it from the shell, but leave it laying in the shell.

Very finely chop three slices of the ginger and combine with the chopped red chili pepper, garlic, light soy sauce and sesame and corn oils. Spoon the sauce evenly over the scallops, then arrange the shells in a tiered steamer.

Bring water to a boil in the bottom of the steamer and scatter in the remaining ginger slices, the rice wine and cilantro (reserving some small leaves for garnish). Steam the scallops for about 6 minutes, until tender.

Garnish with cilantro leaves and serve.

Spicy Prawns Braised in Their Shells

SERVES 4

1 pound 10 ounces medium-sized raw (green) prawns in their shells

¾ cup vegetable oil

3 ounces finely diced fatty bacon (streaked with fat and loin)

2½ tablespoons chili bean paste

1 tablespoon chopped ginger

1 tablespoon chopped garlic

1 teaspoon granulated white sugar

1 cup chicken stock (page 242) or prawn-head stock (page 243)

1 tablespoon rice wine

1 teaspoon soy sauce

3 spring onions (green parts only), finely sliced

1 teaspoon Chinese black vinegar

steamed white rice or thick wheat noodles, to serve

Use kitchen scissors to trim off the prawn legs and the sharp point of the head. With a sharp knife, cut along the center back of each prawn and remove the dark vein.

Heat half the vegetable oil in a wok over very high heat and cook the prawns for about 45 seconds on each side, until the shells are red and crisp. Transfer to a plate.

Carefully pour vegetable oil out of the wok and wipe out the wok with paper towels. Reheat the wok with the remaining vegetable oil over high heat and fry the bacon for 20 seconds. Add the chili bean paste, ginger and garlic, and stir-fry for 30 seconds. Return the prawns to the wok and add the sugar, stock, rice wine and soy sauce. Simmer over high heat for about 5 minutes, then stir in the spring-onions greens and Chinese black vinegar.

Serve with steamed white rice or thick wheat noodles.

✳ This dish can be cooked and served in a clay pot if desired.

Chicken, Quail & Duck

In Chinese cuisine, chicken is simmered, poached or braised just long enough to cook the meat through, leaving a tinge of pink remaining around the bones. Duck, on the other hand, is usually braised slowly until the meat is literally falling off the bones.

With its mild taste and tender flesh, chicken can be paired with just about any Chinese sauce or seasoning, from piquant to delicate. Rich, fatty duck is better teamed with robust seasonings such as Sichuan pepper or chili bean paste, and with strongly flavored ingredients like bamboo shoots or shiitake mushrooms. Recipes for chicken and duck stir-fries can be found in the stir-fries section (pages 78–85).

Quail, goose, pigeon and 'rice bird' (a small sparrow-like bird that invades rice paddies) all feature in Chinese cooking, quail being the most accessible to western cooks.

< PEKING DUCK PANCAKES (PAGE 154)

Peking Duck Pancakes
Bei jing ya bing

PANCAKES
2 ½ cups all-purpose flour,
plus more to flour board
½ teaspoon salt
1 cup boiling water
vegetable oil, to oil hands and
pan
sesame oil, for brushing

FILLING
1 Chinese roast duck
1 small English (seedless)
cucumber, cut into thin
2 ¼-inch strips
4 spring onions, cut into thin
2 ¼-inch strips
Peking duck sauce (page 237)
or hoisin sauce

To make the pancakes, sift all-purpose flour and salt into a bowl and make a well in the center. Pour in the boiling water, stirring quickly to incorporate.

With oiled hands, shape the hot dough into a smooth ball. Place on a board, cover with the bowl and leave for a few minutes to allow the dough to soften and cool. When cool enough to handle, knead to a smooth dough.

Roll the dough out into a long sausage shape and cut into 18 equal pieces. Keep remainder covered with a damp cloth while rolling out each piece to a round about 2 inches in diameter. Brush one side of a round with sesame oil, then press another round on top of it and roll out on a lightly floured board until quite thin and about 6 inches in diameter. Repeat with remaining rounds.

Heat a non-stick fry pan and carefully rub the surface with a piece of paper towel that's been dipped in vegetable oil. Cook the double pancakes for 1½–2 minutes on each side, then carefully separate the two layers and stack the pancakes. Refrigerate, covered, until needed.

For the filling, debone the duck and cut or tear the meat into strips about 2¼ inches × ⅜ inches.

Wrap the pancakes in aluminum foil and warm in the oven, or microwave briefly, then cut each in half.

Arrange a few pieces of cucumber, spring onions and duck on each pancake, add about ⅓ teaspoon peking duck or hoisin sauce, then roll up and arrange on a serving platter.

✳ A purchased roast duck makes an easy and impressive meal. Serve these pancakes as a first course, then use the remaining meat to make a stir-fry with bean sprouts (page 85). The neck and bones can be cooked in a soup for another day (for example the duck & shiitake soup with egg noodles, page 68).

✳ The unfilled pancakes can be made in advance and stored in the refrigerator, tightly wrapped in food wrap, or frozen. Warm in the oven or microwave before use.

✳ You can buy the pancakes from Asian grocers if you don't have time to make them yourself.

Crisp Wok-fried Quail with Chili Pepper & Chinese Pepper—Salt

SERVES 4

4 quail
boiling water, to tighten quail skin
3 spring onions
4 thick slices fresh ginger
vegetable oil for deep-frying

2 tablespoons Sichuan pepper—salt (page 240)
1 fresh hot red chili pepper, deseeded and finely chopped
steamed rice or crisp-fried rice vermicelli, to serve

Place the quail on a wire rack over the sink and slowly pour a pot fill of boiling water over them. (This process tightens the skin, making it crisper when fried.) Leave for 1 hour to drain and dry.

Finely chop half the spring onions and insert the remainder, roughly chopped, into the cavities of the quails. Insert a slice of ginger into each cavity, then close the opening with toothpicks.

Heat the vegetable oil to 350°F. Cook the quail for about 5 minutes, until the skin is golden brown and meat is pink and tender. Remove and drain well on a wire rack. When cool enough to handle, cut each quail in half and discard the spring onion and ginger. Season the skin lightly with some of the sichuan pepper—salt.

Carefully pour the vegetable oil out of the wok (but do not wipe it out). Reheat the wok over high heat and stir-fry the red chili pepper and remaining chopped spring onions for 30 seconds. Add the quail and remaining sichuan pepper—salt and toss until quail is hot.

Serve at once over steamed rice or crisp-fried rice vermicelli.

Steamed Chicken & Mushrooms

Zheng ji gu

SERVES 3–4

1 pound chicken thigh fillets, diced

5 spring onions (white parts only), cut into ¾-inch lengths

5 ounces fresh shiitake or oyster mushrooms, or 1 (15-ounce) can straw mushrooms, drained and cut in half

2 large thin slices fresh ginger, finely shredded

1½ tablespoons light soy sauce

2 teaspoons rice wine

⅓ teaspoon salt

⅓ teaspoon superfine (bar) sugar

1 tablespoon peanut oil

3 tablespoons chicken stock (page 242) or water

simmering water, to steam chicken

1¼ teaspoons cornstarch

cold water, to mix with cornstarch

chopped fresh cilantro or spring-onion greens, for garnish

Combine all the ingredients (except cornstarch and garnish) in a shallow bowl. Set the bowl in a steamer over simmering water, cover, and steam for about 30 minutes, until the chicken is tender.

Strain the liquid into a wok. Mix the cornstarch with about 2 tablespoons cold water and stir into the sauce. Simmer until the sauce thickens and becomes translucent.

Pour the sauce over the chicken and mushrooms, and garnish with fresh cilantro or spring-onion greens.

Soy-braised Chicken
Hong shao ji

SERVES 4–5

4 spring onions
1 (3 pound 5-ounce) chicken
1½-inch piece fresh ginger, cut
   in half
1 cup light soy sauce
½ cup dark soy sauce
½ cup rice wine
½ cup superfine (bar) sugar

¹/₃ teaspoon fennel seeds,
   lightly crushed
1 cinnamon stick
2 star anise
steamed or fried rice and green
   vegetables, to serve

Discard the top half of the spring onions. Cut remainder of each spring onion in half. Place half the spring onions in the cavity of the chicken, along with one chunk of ginger.

Combine remaining ingredients in a saucepan large enough to snugly fit the chicken. Bring to a boil. Put the chicken in the pot, cover, and reduce heat so the liquid simmers gently. Cook for 25 minutes, then remove pot from the heat and leave the chicken in the liquid an additional 20 minutes to finish cooking.

Cut the chicken into serving pieces, using a cleaver to chop straight through the bones. Discard whole spices. Serve with some of the cooking liquid spooned over, with steamed or fried rice and green vegetables.

Tea-smoked Chicken

SERVES 4–5

1 soy-braised chicken
  (page 160)
1½ tablespoons granulated
  white or raw sugar
1½ tablespoons jasmine tea
  leaves
2 tablespoons glutinous (sweet
  sticky) rice

When preparing the soy-braised chicken, remove the chicken from the cooking liquid as soon as the pot is taken off the heat and place it on a wire rack over a tray to drain.

Line an iron wok with a double thickness of aluminum foil. Combine the sugar, jasmine tea leaves and glutinous rice in the wok and place a wire rack on top. Cover the wok and place over a high flame until the ingredients just begin to smoke. Reduce the heat, then place the chicken on the wire rack in the wok, cover, and cook for 6 minutes. Turn the chicken, then cook an additional 6 minutes.

Lift chicken out and place on a cutting board. Chop into bite-sized pieces, using a cleaver to chop straight through the bones, and arrange on a platter.

White-poached Chicken

Bai shao ji

SERVES 4–5

1 (3 pound 5-ounce) chicken
1⅔ quarts chicken stock (page 242)
salt

2 tablespoons finely chopped fresh ginger
2 tablespoons finely chopped spring onion
½ cup vegetable oil, heated

Rinse and drain the chicken. Pour the chicken stock into a deep saucepan, add a little salt and bring to a boil. Reduce heat and simmer for 5 minutes. Add the chicken and bring back to a boil. Skim the chicken stock, then reduce to a gentle simmer and cook for 20 minutes.

Remove the pot from the heat and leave the chicken in the chicken stock for about 10 minutes, until cooked through. (The chicken is done when the thigh feels firm and springs to the touch when pressed.) Lift the chicken onto a tray. Once cool, chop into bite-sized pieces – use a cleaver to chop straight through the bones, or debone the bird first if preferred.

Combine the ginger and spring onion in a bowl. Heat the vegetable oil in a small saucepan, pour it over the ginger and spring onion, and season with salt.

Spoon the vegetable oil mixture over the chicken to serve, or offer it in small dishes for dipping.

Salt-roasted Chicken

Yan jiu ji

SERVES 4–5

1 (3 pound 5-ounce) chicken
¹/₃ cup (peanut or vegetable oil
6 pounds 10 ounces rock salt
1 spring onion, finely chopped

3 thin slices fresh ginger, finely
  chopped
¹/₃ teaspoon salt

Rinse and dry the chicken, then brush all over with peanut or vegetable oil. Wrap the chicken in parchment (baking) paper and set aside.

Line a wok with a double thickness of aluminum foil and add the rock salt. Cover and place over high heat, stirring with a wooden spoon until the salt begins to color and crackle. Make a well in the hot salt and position the chicken into it. Carefully cover the chicken with salt, then cover the wok and reduce heat to medium. Cook for 20 minutes, then carefully scrape off the top layer of salt, turn the chicken, and cook an additional 20 minutes.

Lift the chicken onto a cutting board and unwrap, brushing off all the salt. Cover loosely with aluminum foil and let rest for 10 minutes. Chop the chicken into bite-sized pieces, using a cleaver to chop straight through the bones, or debone the chicken and tear the meat into strips.

In a small bowl, whisk the remaining peanut or vegetable oil with the spring onion, ginger and salt. Serve as a dipping sauce with the chicken.

Crispy Skin Chicken

Ciu pi ji

SERVES 4–5

1 (3 pound 5-ounce) chicken
boiling water, to tighten
    chicken skin
1 teaspoon salt
¾ teaspoon Chinese five-spice
    powder
3 tablespoons maltose

½ cup rice vinegar
water, to prepare syrup
1⅔ quarts vegetable oil for
    deep-frying
Sichuan pepper–salt (page
    240), to serve

Tie the chicken's legs together with kitchen string and hang the bird over a sink or drip tray for 1 hour. (If kitchen is hot, direct a fan onto the chicken to keep it cool while drying.)

Place the chicken on a wire rack set over the sink and carefully pour a kettleful of boiling water over it. Hang the chicken for another hour (again using the fan if necessary to keep it cool), then pour over boiling water again. This process tightens the skin, making it crisper when fried.

Season the cavity of the chicken with the salt and Chinese five-spice powder. **>**

In a small saucepan, combine the maltose, rice vinegar and ⅓ cup water, and heat gently until syrupy. Brush the syrup thickly over the chicken, then hang the bird for another 20 minutes. Repeat the glazing twice more, then let hang until the skin feels dry.

Heat the vegetable oil in a wok to 375°F, then reduce to 360°F.

Carefully lower the dry chicken into the vegetable oil. Cook for about 8 minutes, ladling the vegetable oil very carefully over the top so the chicken cooks evenly. When the chicken is ready, the skin will be red–gold and coming away from the flesh, and the flesh will be firm and pink.

Carefully lift the chicken out of the wok and set on a wire rack over a tray to rest and drain for 10 minutes.

Chop the chicken into serving pieces, using a cleaver to chop straight through the bones, and arrange on a serving plate.

Serve with Sichuan pepper–salt for dipping.

❋ Maltose is the thick, brown, syrupy ingredient that gives Chinese chicken and duck their crisp golden skin. It is sold in Asian food stores, but can be replaced with 2 to 3 tablespoons honey.

Spicy Fried Chicken Drumsticks

SERVES 4

8 small chicken drumsticks
2 teaspoons dark soy sauce
1 tablespoon light soy sauce
1 tablespoon rice wine
2 teaspoons sesame oil
3 teaspoons crushed ginger
½ teaspoon ground Sichuan
  pepper

½ cup cornstarch
½ cup all-purpose flour
2 eggs, well beaten
vegetable oil, for deep-frying
five-spice salt (page 246),
  Sichuan pepper–salt (page
  240) or sweet and sour sauce
  (page 236), for dipping

Place the chicken drumsticks in a bowl and add the dark and light soy sauces, rice wine, sesame oil, ginger and ground sichuan pepper. Mix well, cover, and refrigerate for at least 2 hours.

Combine the cornstarch with the all-purpose flour. Pat the drumsticks dry with paper towels, then coat lightly with the flour mixture. Dip drumsticks into beaten eggs, then coat again with the flour mixture.

Heat vegetabe oil for deep-frying in a wok to 350°F. Fry the drumsticks for about 6 minutes, until golden brown and cooked through.

Serve hot with five-spice salt, Sichuan pepper–salt, or sweet and sour sauce for dipping.

Barbecued Chicken Wings
Kao yang ji

SERVES 4–6 AS A STARTER

12 chicken wings

1 teaspoon salt

¼ teaspoon ground white
  pepper

¼ teaspoon ground chili
  powder

¼ teaspoon ground Sichuan
  pepper

1 spring onion, finely chopped

1 teaspoon grated garlic

2 tablespoons sesame oil

Cut the chicken wings at the joint between the shoulder part and the wing.

Combine remaining ingredients in a bowl, add the chicken pieces and mix well. Cover and marinate for 2–3 hours, or overnight.

Preheat barbecue grill to hot.

Thread wings onto skewers (if desired) and grill for 4–6 minutes, until golden brown and cooked through.

Braised Duck

Hong shao ya lei

SERVES 4–6

1 (4-pound) duck
½ cup dark soy sauce
vegetable oil, for deep-frying
½ cup light soy sauce
½ cup rice wine
3 tablespoons hoisin sauce
½ cup granulated white sugar
2 star anise
1 small piece cassia bark, or a
   1¼-inch piece cinnamon
   stick
½ teaspoon fennel seeds

3 pieces dried mandarin peel,
   or 2 strips orange zest
8 dried shiitake mushrooms,
   soaked in hot water for
   25 minutes
4 spring onions (white parts
   only), roughly chopped
water, to cover and cook duck
1½ teaspoons cornstarch
water, to mix with cornstarch
steamed white rice, to serve

Cut the duck into 8–12 portions, then brush with dark soy sauce and place on a rack to dry for about 20 minutes.

Heat the vegetable oil to 350°F. Cook the duck, a few pieces at a time, until well browned.

Transfer the duck to a casserole dish or saucepan and add the remaining dark soy sauce, the light soy sauce, rice wine, hoisin sauce, sugar, star anise, cassia bark or cinnamon stick, fennel seeds, mandarin peel or orange zest, mushrooms and spring onions. Pour in enough water to barely cover, bring to a boil and reduce heat to low. Simmer very gently, covered, for at least 1 hour, or until the duck is falling off the bones. Carefully transfer the duck to a serving dish.

Skim any excess fat from the braising surface, and strain about 1½ cups of the sauce into a small saucepan. Mix the cornstarch with 3 tablespoons water and pour it into the sauce. Simmer, stirring, until the sauce is thickened and translucent.

Pour sauce over the duck and serve with steamed white rice.

✳ Cassia bark (gui pi) is very similar in flavor to cinnamon and is purchased as flat brown chips.

✳ Mandarin peel is also called tangerine peel. Like cassia bark, mandarin peel can be purchased from Asian markets and herbal speciality shops

Sichuan Spicy Duck Clay Pot

La shao ya sar po

SERVES 2–4

2 duck marylands (entire leg of thigh and drumstick)

3 teaspoons light soy sauce

2 teaspoons dark soy sauce

2 teaspoons rice wine

2 teaspoons cornstarch

2 cups vegetable oil

¾-inch piece fresh ginger, finely chopped

3 cloves garlic, finely chopped

4 spring onions (white parts only), cut into 1½-inch lengths

2 teaspoons Chinese red vinegar

3 teaspoons chili bean paste

1–2 teaspoons granulated white sugar

½–¾ teaspoon Sichuan peppercorns, lightly crushed

2 cups chicken stock (page 242) or duck stock

small sprigs fresh cilantro, for garnish

Place the duck marylands in a bowl and add the light and dark soy sauces, rice wine and cornstarch. Mix well and set aside to marinate for 30 minutes.

Heat the vegetable oil in a wok to 375°F. Pat the duck dry with paper towels. Fry one maryland at a time, until browned. Transfer all the pieces to a clay pot or flameproof casserole dish.

Carefully pour vegetable oil from the wok and wipe out the wok with paper towels.

Return 2 tablespoons of the vegetable oil to the wok and place over high heat. Stir-fry the ginger, garlic and spring onions for 30 seconds. Add the Chinese vinegar, chili bean paste, sugar and sichuan peppercorns, and fry briefly. Pour in the chicken or duck stock and bring to a boil.

Pour the sauce over the duck and simmer, tightly covered, for about 40 minutes, until tender.

Garnish with cilantro and serve in the pot.

✳ Chinese red vinegar is a sweet and tart red rice vinegar, available at Chinese specialty shops.

Pork, Lamb & Beef

In China, more pork is eaten than any other meat. It is added sliced to stir-fries and soups, minced for dumplings, meatballs and snacks, roasted until amber-red and crackling for celebrations, and slow simmered with spices and pungent seasonings for stews and braises. Pork belly and other secondary cuts like pork neck and hocks are enjoyed for their soft, almost gelatinous texture.

Lamb is the prefered meat of Muslim communities of the south, far west and northern regions. Spicy kebabs, skewers and grills feature on many menus and beckon from street-side vendors.

Beef does not feature extensively in Chinese cooking, although it can be used in place of pork and lamb in many dishes.

<PEARL BALLS (PAGE 178)

Pearl Balls

Jun jiu kau

SERVES 4

2 tablespoons dried shrimp, soaked in hot water for 20 minutes

water, to prepare shrimp mixture

1 pound 2 ounces minced pork

2 egg whites

½ spring onion, chopped

1 thin slice fresh ginger

1¼ tablespoons light soy sauce

1½ tablespoons cornstarch

⅓ teaspoon salt

⅓ teaspoon ground white pepper

boiling water, to cook pearl balls

2 cups glutinous (sweet sticky) rice

Chinese greens or other vegetables, to serve

Drain the shrimp and place in a food processor or blender with 1½ tablespoons water and all the remaining ingredients (except rice). Grind until very well mixed and slightly sticky.

With wet hands, mold the shrimp and pork mixture into walnut-sized balls. Spread the glutinous rice on a tray. Roll the balls in the glutinous rice to coat evenly.

Set the glutinous rice-covered balls on plates that will fit in a tiered steamer and fill the base of the steamer with boiling water. Place the plates of glutinous rice covered balls in the steamer, cover, and steam for 25 minutes, until rice is tender.

Serve hot with Chinese greens or other vegetables.

Red Roast Pork
Cha siu

SERVES 6

2 tablespoons honey

2 tablespoons light soy sauce

2 teaspoons dark soy sauce

3 tablespoons hoisin sauce

½ teaspoon Chinese five-spice
powder

1½ tablespoons rice wine

2 tablespoons vegetable oil,
plus extra for brushing

2 pounds 10 ounces pork fillet
or neck, cut into strips
1½ inch thick

Mix the honey, light and dark soy sauces, hoisin sauce, Chinese five-spice powder and rice wine in a bowl with the vegetable oil. Add the pork strips and turn until evenly coated. Cover and marinate for at least 3 hours, or overnight, turning occasionally.

Line a roasting tray with aluminum foil and place in the oven beneath an oven rack. Brush the oven rack with vegetable oil. Preheat the oven to 465°F.

Place the pork strips directly on the oiled oven rack and roast for 25 minutes. Pierce pork strips with a skewer to check for doneness: if the juices run clear, it's ready; if the juices are pink, roast for a few minutes more. Remove pork strips from the oven and transfer to a plate. Cover, and rest for 1 hour before serving.

The pork will keep, wrapped in wax paper or aluminum foil, for 3–4 days in the refrigerator.

Sweet & Sour Pork

SERVES 4

1 pound 2 ounces pork belly,
  skin removed
1 tablespoon light soy sauce
1 cup cornstarch
1 quart 2 ounces vegetable oil,
  for deep-frying
1 quantity sweet and sour sauce
  (page 236)

2 slices fresh or canned
  pineapple, diced
½ cup diced cucumber
½ cup diced onion, blanched
  in boiling water
steamed white rice, to serve

Cut the pork into 3⁄8 inch slices, then cut into bite-sized pieces. Place in a bowl and season with the light soy sauce, then coat thickly with cornstarch.

Heat the vegetable oil to 350°F. Fry the pork, in two or three batches, until golden brown. Remove with a slotted spoon and drain on paper towels.

In a non-stick fry pan, bring the sweet and sour sauce to a boil. Add the pineapple, cucumber and onion, and simmer for about 40 seconds.

Reheat the vegetable oil to 375°F. Fry all of the pork together for about 1½ minutes, until golden and crisp. Remove with a slotted spoon and add to the sauce. Simmer briefly.

Serve with steamed white rice.

Clay-pot Pork with Salted Cabbage & Taro

Su yuk

SERVES 6

1 pound 9 ounces pork belly or neck
cold water, to cover and cook pork
4 ounces salt-pickled cabbage, soaked in cold water for 1 hour
3 teaspoons granulated white sugar
3 cups vegetable oil
1 tablespoon dark soy sauce
1½ cups diced taro
lightly salted boiling water, to cook taro
2 spring onions, chopped
2 tablespoons light soy sauce
water, to prepare sauce
salt or soy sauce (if needed)
steamed white rice, to serve

Place the pork in a saucepan and cover with cold water. Bring to a boil, then reduce heat and simmer for about 40 minutes. Lift the pork onto a wire rack set over a bowl and let drain.

Drain the cabbage and chop roughly. Add half the sugar and 1 tablespoon of the remaining vegetable oil, then spread in a clay pot or flameproof casserole.

Brush the pork with the dark soy sauce, then cut into 1½-inch chunks and set aside for a few minutes to dry. >

Cook the taro in lightly salted boiling water for 10 minutes, and drain.

Heat the remaining vegetable oil in a wok to 350°F. Deep-fry the pork for about 4 minutes, until it is golden brown and the skin is bubbly. Remove from the vegetable oil with a slotted spoon and arrange over the cabbage.

Deep-fry the taro for 1 minute, stirring slowly. Remove and arrange over the pork. Scatter half the spring onions on top and sprinkle with the remaining sugar. Pour in the light soy sauce and ¾ cup water. Cover tightly and cook very gently on the stove top – or in a 325°F oven – for about 1 hour, stirring once or twice. Add a little extra water during cooking if the dish seems dry (but it is not intended to have much sauce). Check for seasoning, adding salt or extra soy sauce if needed.

Serve in the pot, garnished with remaining spring onions, with steamed white rice alongside.

✳ Taro is a starchy root vegetable with firm, dry flesh that is cream to grey in color (the thick brown skin is inedible). White sweet potato, parsnip, yam, or new potatoes can replace the taro, but may require adjusted cooking time.

Simmered Pork
Bai shao zhurou

SERVES 4–6

2 pound 3 ounces pork neck or
  belly
boiling water, to cover and cold
  water to cook pork
2 teaspoons salt

1¼-inch piece fresh ginger,
  thickly sliced
1 spring onion, cut into
  ¾-inch lengths

Place the pork in a saucepan and cover with boiling water. Drain at once. Return pork to the saucepan and pour in enough cold water to cover. Add the salt, ginger and spring onion, and bring to a boil. Reduce heat and simmer for about 25 minutes.

Remove saucepan from the heat and let the pork rest in the hot stock an additional 20 minutes to finish cooking. Lift pork out of the pan and drain on a wire rack.

Simmered pork will keep for at least 5 days in the refrigerator.

✳ Hot or cold simmered pork can be sliced or chopped and added to stir-fries, fried rice, noodle dishes or soups. Try it in these two delicious recipes: sliced pork with garlic sauce (page 19) and twice-cooked pork with bell pepper and chili (page 86).

Braised Pork Ribs with Black Beans, Garlic & Chili Pepper

SERVES 5–6

3 pounds pork spare ribs

4 spring onions, chopped

¾-inch piece ginger, roughly chopped

2–3 fresh hot red chili peppers, deseeded and chopped

5 cloves garlic, chopped

3 tablespoons salted (Chinese fermented) black beans, chopped

2 tablespoons dark soy sauce

½ cup light soy sauce

3 tablespoons rice wine

3 tablespoons granulated white sugar

water, to prepare sauce

steamed white rice and Chinese greens, to serve

Preheat the oven to 350°F.

Use a cleaver to chop the pork spare ribs into 2-inch chunks. Place in a single layer in a casserole dish and scatter with the spring onions, ginger, red chili peppers, garlic and salted black beans. Mix the light and dark soy sauces, rice wine and sugar with ½ cup water, and pour it over the pork spare ribs. Cover the dish and bake for 1 hour. Turn the pork spare ribs and cook an additional 20 minutes, then uncover, turn again and cook until browned.

Serve with steamed white rice and Chinese greens.

Sizzling Lamb & Onions

SERVES 3–4

1 pound lamb backstrap or
   fillet, thinly sliced
2 tablespoons light soy sauce
2 teaspoons dark soy sauce
1½ tablespoons sesame oil
1 tablespoon rice wine
2 tablespoons hoisin sauce
¾ teaspoon Chinese five-spice
   powder
1½ teaspoons granulated white
   sugar

3 teaspoons sesame seeds,
   reserve for garnish
2 tablespoons vegetable oil
2 medium-sized onions, finely
   sliced
1 green bell pepper, cut into
   thin strips (optional)
fried rice or steamed white
   rice, to serve

Place the lamb in a bowl and add the light and dark soy sauces, half the sesame oil, rice wine, hoisin sauce, Chinese five-spice powder and sugar. Mix well and marinate for 1 hour, or overnight.

Preheat the oven to 425°F, placing a heavy iron plate or ovenproof fry pan in the oven to heat.

Heat a wok, without vegetable oil, and toast the sesame seeds until golden. Place into a bowl to cool. Reserve for garnish.

Reheat the wok with the vegetable oil over high heat. Stir-fry the onions and bell pepper (if using) for about 2½ minutes, until almost cooked. Place onto a plate.

Reheat the wok over very high heat, then add the remaining sesame oil and the marinated lamb slices and stir-fry for about 45 seconds. (It is important not to overcook the lamb slices.)

Remove the iron plate or oven proof fry pan from the oven and spread the onions and bell pepper over it. Arrange the lamb slices evenly on top and scatter with the sesame seeds.

Serve at once, with fried rice or steamed white rice.

✳ Lamnb backstrap, also known as lamb fillet, is cut from the eye muscle that lies along the spine.

Mongolian Barbecue Lamb
Shuan yang rou

SERVES 4

2 pounds 2 ounces lamb
    shoulder, partially frozen
1½-inch piece fresh young
    ginger
1 tablespoon rice wine
⅓ cup light soy sauce
1 tablespoon granulated white
    sugar

2½ teaspoons sesame oil
6 spring onions
vegetable oil, to wipe hotplate
    or fry pan
rice or warmed pocket bread,
    to serve

Cut the lamb into paper-thin slices and arrange on a plate. Grate the ginger onto a clean piece of cheesecloth and squeeze the juice into a bowl. Add the rice wine, light soy sauce, sugar and sesame oil, and mix well.

Cut the spring onions into 2-inch lengths, then shred lengthwise.

To serve, heat a tabletop hotplate or electric fry pan (or use a large non-stick fry pan set over a portable gas burner). When the hotplate or fry pan is very hot, carefully wipe the surface with a paper towel dipped in vegetable oil.

To eat, diners use wooden chopsticks to dip slices of lamb into the sauce and then place them on the hotplate or fry pan to cook for barely a minute. The spring onions are cooked alongside.

Serve with rice or warmed pocket bread.

✳ Freeze the lamb until firm enough to cut into extremely thin slices.

Crisp Fried Sesame Beef

Niurou bao

SERVES 2–4

12 ounce beef fillet

½ cup cornstarch, plus additional to thicken sauce

2 tablespoons sesame seeds

vegetable oil, for deep-frying

¾ cup chicken stock (page 242)

1 tablespoon sesame oil

2 teaspoons finely chopped fresh ginger

2 teaspoons finely chopped garlic

1 teaspoon dark soy sauce

1 teaspoon Chinese black vinegar

1 teaspoon granulated white sugar, or to taste

steamed vegetables and steamed white or fried rice, to serve

Cut the beef into thin slices, then spread out over a sheet of parchment (baking) paper or heavy food wrap, leaving space between each piece. Cover with another sheet of parchment paper or food wrap and gently tap with the flat side of a meat cleaver or a rolling pin to flatten the beef until very thin (almost transparent). Coat the beef lightly with cornstarch, shaking off the excess.

Heat a wok, without vegetable oil, over medium heat and toast the sesame seeds until golden. Place into a bowl, and reserve.

Heat the vegetable oil for deep-frying to 375°F. Fry the beef, about six pieces at a time, for 40 seconds or until crisp. Drain on a rack set over paper towels. Turn off heat and carefully pour all but 1 tablespoon vegetable oil from the wok. **>**

Combine the chicken stock and 2/3 teaspoon cornstarch in a bowl. Set aside.

Reheat the wok over high heat and add the sesame oil. Stir-fry the ginger and garlic for about 30 seconds, then add the dark soy sauce, Chinese black vinegar, sugar to taste, stock and cornstarch mixture and sesame seeds. Simmer, stirring, until the sauce thickens. Return the beef slices to the wok and stir to heat through and coat with the sauce.

Serve at once, with green vegetables and steamed white rice or fried rice.

✳ Chinese black vinegar is made from glutinous (sweet sticky rice), millet or sorghum. It has a deep, almost smoky flavor. Balsamic vinegar can substitute.

Barbecue Lamb Skewers

SERVES 4

1 pound 5 ounces lean lamb
1¼ teaspoons salt
½ teaspoon freshly ground
   black pepper
¼ teaspoon ground Sichuan
   pepper

½ spring onion, finely
   chopped
1 teaspoon grated ginger
1 tablespoon light soy sauce
1 tablespoon sesame oil

Cut the lamb into thin slices, then into 1¼-inch long strips. Combine the remaining ingredients in a bowl, add the lamb and mix well. Cover and marinate for 3–4 hours, or overnight.

Thread strips of lamb onto metal skewers (or use bamboo skewers that have been soaked in water for 30 minutes).

Preheat a barbecue grill to hot.

Grill the lamb skewers for 4–6 minutes, turning often, until crisp and browned on the outside but still slightly pink inside.

Beef Braised with Red Dates

SERVES 6

2 pounds 3 ounces beef brisket, cut into 2¼-inch cubes

8–12 dried red dates

8 paper-thin slices fresh ginger

3 spring onions (white parts only), cut into 1¼-inch pieces

3 pieces dried mandarin (or tangerine) peel

1½ tablespoons rice wine

2 tablespoons dark soy sauce, plus extra if needed

boiling water, to cover beef

salt (if needed)

1 teaspoon granualted white sugar (if needed)

steamed white rice or soft noodles, to serve

Place the beef cubes in a wok, cover with lukewarm water, then bring to a boil. Reduce heat and simmer for 5 minutes. Drain.

Transfer the beef cubes to a clay pot or heavy saucepan and add the dried dates, ginger, spring onions, mandarin or tangerine peel, rice wine and dark soy sauce. Pour in enough boiling water to cover. Cover the pot, bring to a boil, then reduce to a simmer and cook gently for about 1½ hours. Check for seasoning, adding salt or extra soy sauce if needed. Add a teaspoon of sugar if needed. Cook an additional 30 minutes or until the beef is very tender.

Serve over steamed white rice or soft noodles.

✳ Lamb shoulder or leg can replace the beef brisket.

✳ Red dates are also called Chinese Korean or Indian dates and jujubes. They are available at Asian specialty food stores. Substitute dried dates, apples, prunes, or raisins.

Braised Beef Brisket

SERVES 6

2 tablespoons vegetable oil

2 pounds 3 ounces beef brisket,
cut into 1½-inch cubes

2 star anise

1 teaspoon Sichuan
peppercorns

½ teaspoon black peppercorns

2 cloves garlic, peeled

1¾ ounces ginger, sliced

2 tablespoons soy-bean paste

water, to cover and cook brisket

1 tablespoon oyster sauce

2 teaspoons dark soy sauce

2 tablespoons light soy sauce

1 tablespoon rice wine

½–2 teaspoons granulated
white sugar

2 tablespoons cornstarch

cold water, to mix with
cornstarch

steamed white rice, to serve

Heat the vegetable oil in a fry pan and brown the beef brisket. Transfer the beef brisket cubes to a clay pot or flameproof casserole and add the spices, garlic, ginger and soy-bean paste, and cook briefly. Pour in enough water to cover and bring to a boil. Reduce heat and simmer for about 1 hour. Remove pot or casserole from the heat and let the beef brisket cubes rest in the broth for 1 hour. Then bring back to a boil, add the oyster sauce, and dark and light soy sauces, rice wine and sugar to taste, and simmer for another 30 minutes.

Stir the cornstarch into a couple of tablespoons of cold water and pour half of the mixture into the sauce. Simmer, stirring, until the sauce thickens. Add the remaining cornstarch mixture to make a thicker sauce, if desired.

Serve over steamed white rice.

Vegetables & Tofu

Vegetables feature strongly in Chinese cooking, adding vibrant color and appealing texture to stir-fries and noodles, soups and braised dishes. Many vegetable dishes can be served on their own as a vegetarian meal, or as an accompaniment to meat, poultry or seafood.

Many of the most popular Chinese vegetables are now sold at supermarkets, which means bok choy, Chinese cabbage (wombok) and crunchy snow peas can now be used as everyday vegetables.

Numerous vegetable dishes include the important ingredient tofu. Tofu (bean curd) is made by soaking, steaming, grinding and straining yellow soy beans to obtain a creamy milk, which is then firmed with a setting agent. There are a number of varieties. Silken or soft tofu is the most fragile and mild in taste. Firm tofu is obtained by pressing out more water from silken tofu, while fried tofu puffs are cubes of tofu that have been deep-fried.

< STEAMED STUFFED MUSHROOMS (PAGE 202)

Steamed Stuffed Mushrooms

SERVES 4–6

12 large dried shiitake
   mushrooms, soaked in hot
   water for 25 minutes
5 ounces minced chicken
1 spring onion, very finely
   chopped
½ teaspoon finely grated ginger
2 teaspoons light soy sauce
1 teaspoon rice wine

2⅔ teaspoons cornstarch
½–1 egg white, beaten
gently simmering water, to
   steam mushrooms
¾ cup chicken stock (page 242)
1 teaspoon sesame oil
½ teaspoon dark soy sauce

Drain the mushrooms, then trim the tough stems close to the caps.

In a bowl, combine the minced chicken, spring onion, ginger, light soy sauce, rice wine and 2 teaspoons cornstarch. Mix thoroughly. Add enough egg white to make a sticky mixture.

With wet hands, fill each mushroom with stuffing. Arrange, stuffing side up, in a steamer basket and steam over gently simmering water for about 15 minutes, until mushrooms are tender.

Combine the chicken stock, sesame oil, dark soy sauce and remaining cornstarch in a small saucepan and simmer gently, stirring, until the sauce thickens.

Transfer mushrooms to a platter and pour the sauce over. Serve at once.

Steamed Chinese Greens
Zheng cai

SERVES 4–6

2 bunches baby bok choy, gai
    larn or choy sum (or other
    Chinese green vegetables)
2½ tablespoons vegetable oil
water, to steam vegetables

sesame oil, light soy sauce or
    oyster sauce, for drizzling
    (optional)

If using baby bok choy, trim off the lower ends of the stems and cut into halves or quarters if large. For gai larn or choy sum, remove flowers and the woody sections of the stems.

Heat the vegetable oil in a wok over high heat and stir-fry the vegetables until coated with vegetable oil. Add ½ cup water, cover the wok tightly, and steam the vegetables until tender (2–2½ minutes for baby bok choy; 2½–4 minutes for gai larn or choy sum). Drain the vegetables and arrange on a serving dish.

The cooked vegetables can be served with a drizzle of sesame oil, light soy sauce or oyster sauce.

✳ Gai larn is Chinese broccoli or kale. Choy sum is Chinese chard or bok choy.

Combination Stir-fried Vegetables
Chao shu cai lei

SERVES 4

²/₃ cup chicken stock (page 242)

¾ teaspoon cornstarch

lightly salted water, to parboil the vegetables

1 small carrot, thinly sliced

3–4 green beans, cut into 1¼-inch lengths

6–8 small broccoli florets

6–8 small cauliflower florets

2½ tablespoons vegetable oil

1 small onion, 'Asian cut' (see page 10)

½ red bell pepper, cut into ¾-inch squares

4½ ounces fresh baby corn, cut in half or 1 (14½-ounce) can baby corn, drained

3–4 button mushrooms, sliced

¼ cup sliced bamboo shoots or water chestnuts

2 teaspoons rice wine

3 teaspoons light soy sauce, plus more if needed

salt (if needed)

In a small bowl combine the chicken stock and cornstarch. Set aside.

Bring a small saucepan of lightly salted water to a simmer and parboil the carrot, green beans, broccoli and cauliflower for about 1½ minutes. Drain.

Heat the vegetable oil in a wok over high heat and stir-fry the onion and bell pepper for 1 minute. ➤

Add the parboiled vegetables to the wok, along with the fresh baby corn or canned, drained baby corn, mushrooms and bamboo shoots or water chestnuts, and stir-fry on high heat for 1 minute. Season with the rice wine and light soy sauce, and pour in the chicken stock and cornstarch mixture. Simmer, stirring, for 1–2 minutes, until sauce is thickened. Check seasoning, adding salt or more soy sauce if needed.

✳ Asparagus, bok choy, Chinese cabbage (wombok), sliced Brussels sprouts, zucchini or even cucumber could all be used in this tasty vegetable combination.

Lettuce with Oyster Sauce

SERVES 4–5

⅓ cup vegetable oil

3 very thin slices fresh ginger,
   finely shredded

1 small iceberg or cos lettuce,
   roughly torn

1 teaspoon salt

2 tablespoons oyster sauce

Heat the vegetable oil over medium–high heat, add the ginger and fry for 30 seconds. Add the lettuce and stir-fry for about 1 minute, until the leaves wilt. Carefully pour off excess vegetable oil, then add the salt and oyster sauce, and cook an additional 20–30 seconds.

Serve at once.

✳ The large amount of vegetable oil helps prevent the lettuce from turning brown during cooking.

Chinese Cabbage, Bean Sprouts & Oyster Mushrooms

SERVES 4–6

½ head Chinese cabbage (wombok)
5 ounces fresh bean sprouts
boiling water, to blanch bean sprouts
3 tablespoons vegetable oil
4–5 thin slices fresh ginger, finely shredded
water, to steam cabbage stems

3½ ounces oyster mushrooms
5 spring onions, finely sliced on a diagonal
$1/3$ teaspoon salt
$1/3$ teaspoon granulated white sugar
1 tablespoon light soy sauce

Trim off any damaged outer leaves from the cabbage. Roughly chop the curly leaf tops and set aside, then finely slice the thicker white stems.

Blanch the bean sprouts in boiling water, and drain immediately.

Heat the vegetable oil in a wok over high heat, add the ginger and fry briefly. Add the chopped cabbage stems and stir-fry for 30 seconds, then add 2 tablespoons water, cover, and steam for 1 minute. Add the remaining cabbage, bean sprouts, oyster mushrooms, spring onions and salt, sugar, and light soy sauce, and continue to stir-fry until the cabbage is almost tender.

Sichuan Green Beans & Spicy Pork

SERVES 4–6

3½ ounces minced pork
1 teaspoon dark soy sauce
1½ teaspoons granulated white
   sugar
1½ cups vegetable oil
1 pound green beans, cut in
   half

1 spring onion, finely chopped
2–3 teaspoons chili bean paste
1 clove garlic, finely chopped
water, to simmer greens
salt (if needed)

Season the minced pork with the dark soy sauce and ½ teaspoon of the sugar, mixing well to combine.

Heat the vegetable oil in a wok over high heat and fry the green beans for about 1½ minutes, until they are well cooked and beginning to shrivel. Transfer to a plate.

Carefully pour all but 2 tablespoons vegetable oil from the wok. Reheat the wok over high heat, add the minced pork, spring onion, chili bean paste, remaining sugar and garlic, and stir-fry for about 1½ minutes, until the pork is well cooked. Add 3 tablespoons water and return the green beans to the wok. Simmer until the liquid has evaporated. Check seasoning, adding a pinch of salt if needed.

Stir-fried Asparagus & Broccolini with Ginger & Sesame

SERVES 3–4

1 bunch asparagus

1 bunch broccolini

1/3 teaspoon cornstarch

3 tablespoons chicken stock (page 242)

2 tablespoons vegetable oil, divided

5 thin slices fresh ginger

water, to cook asparagus

1½ teaspoons sesame oil

2 teaspoons sesame seeds, divided for garnish

2 teaspoons light soy sauce

Snap off the woody ends of the asparagus and discard. Cut thick asparagus spears diagonally into long slices, or cut thin asparagus spears into 2-inch lengths. Trim the ends of the broccolini, and cut each stem in half.

Combine the cornstarch and chicken stock in a small bowl, and set aside.

Heat half the vegetable oil in a wok over high heat and stir-fry the asparagus, broccolini and ginger for 30 seconds. Add 2 tablespoons water, then cover the wok tightly and cook on high heat for 2 minutes, shaking the wok from time to time. Uncover and carefully pour out any liquid. Add the remaining vegetable oil, the sesame oil and half the sesame seeds, and stir-fry for 30 seconds. Pour in the light soy sauce and the cornstarch and chicken stock mixture, and simmer over high heat until the sauce coats the vegetables.

Serve at once, sprinkled with remaining sesame seeds.

Bell Pepper & Bean Sprout Stir-fry

SERVES 4

½ teaspoon cornstarch

⅓ cup chicken stock (page 242) or water

3 tablespoons vegetable oil

5 ounces bean sprouts

1 teaspoon finely chopped garlic

1 teaspoon finely chopped ginger

1 yellow bell pepper, cut into thin strips

1 green bell pepper, cut into thin strips

1 red bell pepper, cut into thin strips

1 small fresh hot red or green chili pepper, deseeded and chopped

1 small onion, 'Asian cut' (see page 10)

2 teaspoons oyster sauce

2 teaspoons soy sauce

½ teaspoon salt

1 teaspoon granulated white sugar

Stir the cornstarch into the chicken stock or water and set aside.

Heat a wok over very high heat and add 2 teaspoons vegetable oil. Stir-fry the bean sprouts with the garlic and ginger for 30 seconds, then transfer to a plate.

Heat the remaining vegetable oil in the wok and stir-fry the bell peppers, chili pepper and onion for 2 minutes, until softened. Return bean sprouts to the wok and add the oyster and soy sauces, salt and sugar. Pour in the cornstarch and chicken stock or water mixture and cook, stirring, until it glazes the vegetables. Add a little salt, soy sauce or sugar if needed.

Spinach Seasoned with Shrimp Paste

SERVES 3–4

1 bunch Chinese water spinach
　or 2 bunches baby spinach
2½ tablespoons vegetable oil
1¼ teaspoons soft shrimp paste
1½ tablespoons light soy sauce
½ teaspoon granulated white
　sugar

Wash spinach well. If using Chinese water spinach, discard the tough stem ends. Chop spinach leaves roughly, then shake inside a kitchen towel or spin in a salad spinner to remove excess water. If using baby spinach, wash and dry.

Heat the vegetebale oil in a wok over high heat and stir-fry the spinach for about 40 seconds, until it wilts. Add the shrimp paste, light soy sauce and sugar, and toss to mix well.

Serve at once.

Crisp-fried Greens with Candied Cashews

SERVES 3–4

1 large bunch Chinese greens
   (kale, mustard greens, bok
   choy, choy sum)
1/3 cup granulated white sugar
water, to dissolve sugar

2 teaspoons light soy sauce
1 cup raw cashews
2 teaspoons five-spice salt
  (page 246)
2 cups vegetable oil

Trim stems from Chinese greens and discard (or save for another recipe). Stack several leaves together, roll up tightly and shred very finely. Repeat with remaining leaves.

Set aside 1 teaspoon of the sugar and in a small saucepan dissolve the remaining sugar with 1 tablespoon water and the light soy sauce, and cook until the mixture turns golden brown. Quickly add the cashews and 1 teaspoon of the five-spice salt, and swirl to coat the cashews. Place onto a lightly oiled plate to cool.

Heat the vegetable oil in a wok to 350°F. Fry half the shredded leaves until crisp and crackling. Remove with a wire skimmer and place in a colander or on paper towels to drain. Fry the remaining leaves.

Spread all of the crisp greens on a serving plate, sprinkle with the reserved sugar and five-spice salt, and pile the cashews in the center. Serve at once.

Steamed Stuffed Tofu
Zheng doufu

SERVES 4

12 ounces firm tofu
4 ½ ounce minced pork
2 teaspoons chopped cilantro
    leaves
1 tablespoon very finely
    chopped button mushrooms
1 teaspoon cornstarch

1 teaspoon light soy sauce
simmering water, to steam tofu
steamed Chinese greens, to
    serve
1 ½ tablespoons oyster sauce, to
    serve

Cut the tofu into 1 ½-inch squares and use a teaspoon to remove a small scoop of tofu from the top of each square.

Combine the minced pork, cilantro, mushrooms, cornstarch and light soy sauce in a blender or food processor and blend to make a fairly smooth paste. (Alternatively, squeeze the mixture through your fingers to combine it.)

Press a spoonful of pork mixture onto the top of each piece of tofu. Set tofu squares on a plate and place in a steamer over simmering water. Pour over the chicken stock and steam for about 5 minutes.

Serve over steamed Chinese greens, drizzled with oyster sauce.

Braised Bamboo Shoots & Mushrooms

1½ cups peanut oil

2 (15-ounce) cans whole bamboo shoots, cut into ¾-inch chunks

3 slices fresh ginger

2 cloves garlic, peeled

10 dried shiitake mushrooms, soaked in hot water for 25 minutes

3 spring onions (white parts only), cut into 1½-inch pieces

2 cups chicken stock (page 242)

2 teaspoons dark soy sauce

1 tablespoon light soy sauce

2 teaspoons rice wine

½ teaspoon granulated white sugar

salt (if needed)

a few drops of Chinese red vinegar

Heat the vegetable oil in a wok over high heat and fry the bamboo shoots for about 1 minute, until brown. Transfer to a plate. Carefully pour all but 2 tablespoons peanut oil from the wok. Reheat the wok and fry the ginger and garlic for about 40 seconds, then discard the ginger and garlic solids.

Return the bamboo shoots to the wok and add the mushrooms, spring onions, chicken stock, dark and light soy sauces, rice wine and sugar. Bring to a boil, then reduce heat and simmer for about 20 minutes, until mushrooms are tender and the sauce well reduced. Add salt if needed, and sprinkle in the Chinese red vinegar.

Deep-fried Silken Tofu

SERVES 3–4

14 ounce silken tofu
½ cup cornstarch
3 cups vegetable oil
2 tablespoons sesame oil
1½ tablespoons Sichuan
   pepper–salt (page 240)

1 fresh hot red chili pepper,
   deseeded and finely chopped
light soy sauce (optional)

Gently remove the tofu from its container and carefully cut into ¾-inch slices, then cut each slice in half. Pat dry with paper towels and dust lightly with cornstarch.

Heat the vegetable and sesame oils to 350°F in a wok. Carefully slide in the tofu and deep-fry for 1½–2 minutes, until golden brown. Remove tofu with a wire skimmer and drain on paper towels.

Carefully pour the oil from the wok and wipe out the wok with paper towels. Reheat the wok, add the sichuan pepper–salt and hot red chili pepper, and stir over high heat for about 30 seconds.

Sprinkle the sichuan pepper–salt and hot red chili pepper over the tofu, and drizzle with a little light soy sauce if desired. Serve at once.

Mustard Greens & Fried Tofu

Jiecai doufu

SERVES 4

8 pieces deep-fried tofu puffs
boiling water, to cover tofu
1 bunch Chinese mustard
   greens, roughly chopped
boiling water, to cook mustard
   greens
pinch of baking soda
salt, to taste
½ cup vegetable oil
⅔ cup chicken stock (page

242)
2 tablespoons oyster sauce
1 tablespoon light soy sauce
⅔ teaspoon cornstarch
2 thin slices fresh ginger, finely
   chopped
1 large clove garlic, finely
   chopped

Place the deep-fried tofu puffs in a bowl and cover with boiling water. Set aside for 10 minutes.

Place the mustard greens in a saucepan and cover with boiling water. Add baking soda and a pinch of salt, and bring to a boil. Add half the vegetable oil, then reduce heat and simmer for 5–6 minutes, until tender.

Place the mustard greens and tofu puffs into a colander to drain for a few minutes.

In a small bowl combine the chicken stock, oyster and light soy sauces and cornstarch, and set aside.

Heat the remaining vegetable oil in a wok over high heat. Add the ginger and garlic, and fry for 20 seconds. Add the mustard greens and tofu puffs, and stir-fry briefly to coat with vegetable oil, then pour in the chicken stock mixture and simmer gently until the sauce coats the ingredients (about 2 minutes). Add salt to taste.

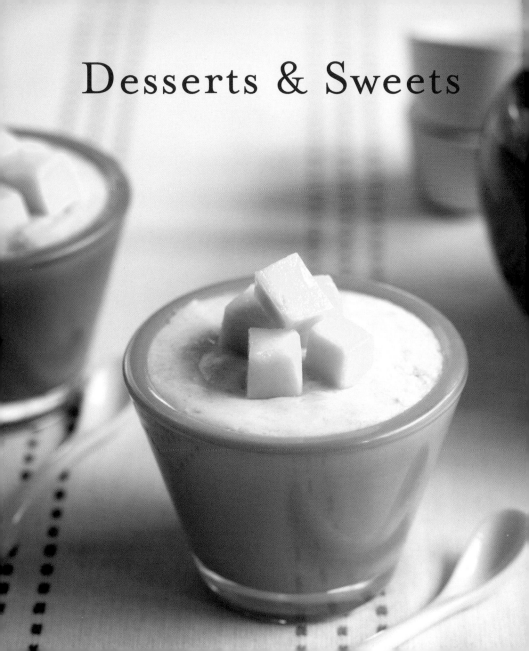

Desserts & Sweets

A plate of sliced fresh fruit is usually served at the end of a Chinese meal. However, many of the sweet dishes served in dim sum restaurants can be enjoyed as desserts at home.

Dairy products rarely feature in Chinese cooking, with nuts, seeds, dried beans and coconut often providing the creaminess in desserts. Products such as sweet red-bean paste, black-sesame paste and lotus-seed paste are used in sweet soups or as fillings for buns and pastries.

The Chinese have a fondness for jellies and soft, silky textures—evident here in the coconut and almond jellies, succulent mango mousse, and soft sweet tofu served with sugar syrup. Peaches and crisp white pears are favorite fruits in China and make elegant desserts.

< MANGO MOUSSE (PAGE 224)

Mango Mousse

SERVES 4–6

2 cups diced mango, fresh or
 frozen (thawed)
1 cup cream
1 tablespoon powdered
 unflavored gelatin

cold water, to soften and
 simmering water to dissolve
 gelatin
3 tablespoons superfine (bar)
 sugar

Place the mango in a food processor or blender and purée until smooth.

Whip the cream to soft peaks.

Add the gelatin and ½ cup cold water to a heatproof bowl and set aside for 5 minutes to allow the gelatine to soften. Set the bowl over a saucepan of simmering
water and stir to dissolve. Add the superfine sugar and stir slowly until it dissolves.

Combine the mango, cream and sweetened gelatin in a bowl, mixing lightly but
thoroughly. Spoon into individual dessert dishes and chill until softly set.

Serve cold.

Coconut Jelly

1 (13½ fluid ounce) can
    coconut cream
1⅓ cups milk
½ cup superfine (bar) sugar
5 teaspoons powdered
    unflavored agar agar
flavorless cooking oil, to oil
    mold
1 cup fine desiccated coconut

Heat the coconut cream, milk and superfine sugar in a saucepan until almost boiling. Stir in the agar agar and simmer gently for 2 minutes.

Pour mixture into a square 3-cup capacity mold that has been lightly oiled with a flavorless cooking oil. Let cool, then refrigerate until set.

Cut the jelly into 1¼-inch cubes and roll in the coconut to coat.

✳ Agar agar is a vegetarian gelatin substitute, available at specialty markets.

✳ Desiccated coconut has been shredded or flaked and dried to remove moisture.

Almond Jelly
Xin ren doufu

SERVES 6

2 ½ cups milk

1 cup soy milk

2 tablespoons powdered
   unflavored agar agar

½ cup superfine (bar) sugar

2–3 teaspoons almond extract,
   to taste

flavorless vegetable oil, to oil
   mold

3 cups diced fresh fruit
   (star fruit, pineapple,
   mangosteen, lychee,
   papayas), to serve

Combine the milk, soy milk, agar agar, superfine sugar and almond extract to taste in a saucepan, and bring to a boil, stirring slowly. Simmer for about 4 minutes over gentle heat, then strain into a 1 quart 2-fluid ounce capacity square mold that has been lightly oiled with a flavorless vegetable oil. Let cool, then refrigerate until set and cold.

Cut the jelly into diamond shapes and serve with diced fruit.

Sweet Tofu
Tian doufu

SERVES 4–6

3 cups soy milk
1¹/₃ cups superfine (bar) sugar
1 tablespoon powdered
    unflavored gelatin
water to prepare sugar syrup

Combine the soy milk and ⅓ cup of the superfine sugar in a saucepan and bring slowly to a boil. Stir in the unflavored gelatin and when dissolved pour mixture into a 1 quart 2-fluid ounce capacity dish. Leave for at least 2 hours, until set into a very soft jelly.

Boil remaining sugar and 1⅓ cups water in a small saucepan for about 8 minutes, then allow to cool to room temperature.

Scoop spoonfuls of the sweet tofu into individual dishes and drizzle with the sugar syrup.

Sweet Red-bean Soup
Lian zi hong dou sha

SERVES 6

1 (15-ounce can) sweet
   red-bean paste
water, to combine with
   red-bean paste
3–5 tablespoons superfine
   (bar) sugar
2 tablespoons chopped roasted
   peanuts, for garnish

Combine the red-bean paste with 1½ cups water in a saucepan, and add superfine sugar to taste. Bring mixture slowly to a boil, stirring continuously. Simmer for 2–3 minutes.

Ladle soup into small bowls and garnish with peanuts. Serve hot.

Poached White Peaches

SERVES 4

4 white peaches
¾ cup Chinese rock sugar
water, to poach peaches
sweet sticky rice or sweet tofu,
   to serve

Peel the peaches. Leave whole, or cut in half and remove the stones.

Combine the superfine sugar with 3 cups water in a saucepan and bring to a boil. Simmer for 5 minutes, until the sugar has completely dissolved, then add the peaches. Reduce the heat and poach gently for 8–10 minutes, until the fruit is tender.

Serve warm or cold, in the syrup, with sweet sticky rice (glutinous rice sweetened with sugar) or sweet tofu (page 228).

✳ Rock (crystal) sugar is often used in Chinese desserts, as it produces a clear syrup with a delicate flavor. It comes in large crystals which are usually crushed with a meat mallet or rolling pin before use. You can use 5 ounces superfine (bar) sugar instead.

Pears in Star-anise Syrup

SERVES 4

4 nashi or other pears
2 star anise
3 thin slices fresh ginger
1/3 cup superfine (bar) sugar
water, to cover and cook pears

Peel the pears, leaving the stems attached. Leave whole or cut in half.

Combine the star anise, ginger and superfine sugar in a saucepan. Add the pears and pour in enough warm water to barely cover. Simmer gently for about 9 minutes, stirring occasionally, until the pears are tender. Remove spices.

Serve warm or cold, in the star-anise syrup.

✳ Nashi (Asian pears) are crunchy, fragrant and juicy. Bosc pears can be substituted.

Stuffed Egg Puffs

MAKES 12

3½ ounce sweet lotus seed
   or chestnut paste, or sweet
   red-bean paste
3 tablespoons cornstarch
8 egg whites
1½ tablespoons all-purpose
   flour

3 cups vegetable oil for deep-
   frying
2 tablespoons sesame oil
1–2 tablespoons superfine (bar)
   sugar or toasted sesame seeds,
   for garnish

Shape the sweet seed or bean paste into 12 round balls. Set 1 tablespoon cornstarch aside and use the remainder to lightly coat the balls.

Whip the egg whites to stiff peaks, then carefully fold in the reserved cornstarch and the all-purpose flour.

Heat the vegetable oil to 375°F, add the sesame oil and reduce to 350°F.

Pierce a sweet ball with a skewer and gently drag it through the meringue mixture to coat thickly.

Carefully slip sweet balls into the oil mixture, two or three at a time, and fry for about 1½ minutes, until golden brown. Remove with a slotted spoon and sprinkle immediately with superfine sugar or toasted sesame seeds. Serve warm.

Extras

Various sauces, stocks and flavored salt mixes are used over and over again in Chinese cooking. Here you'll find recipes for essentials like sweet and sour sauce, garlic dipping sauce and Sichuan pepper–salt. There are also recipes for homemade stock and instructions for how to make perfect steamed white rice.

< SWEET & SOUR SAUCE (PAGE 236), PEKING DUCK SAUCE (PAGE 237) AND GARLIC DIPPING SAUCE (PAGE 238)

Sweet & Sour Sauce

MAKES ABOUT 1¾ CUPS

2 teaspoons cornstarch
water, to mix with cornstarch
²/₃ cupsuperfine (bar) sugar
½ cup rice vinegar
¹/₃ cup tomato sauce
1 teaspoon light soy sauce
water, to simmer ingrdients

Stir the cornstarch into 2 tablespoons water and set aside.

Combine the remaining ingredients in a wok or small saucepan with ½ cup water and simmer for 2 minutes. Pour the cornstarch mixture into the sauce and simmer, stirring slowly, until the sauce thickens (about 1 minute).

Sweet and sour sauce can be stored in the refrigerator for 4–5 days.

✳ This makes a reasonably thin sauce. Use extra cornstarch for a thicker sauce, if preferred.

✳ Diced bell pepper, cucumber, onion or pineapple can be simmered in the sauce for added color and texture. Chopped ginger, chili powder or coriander, or some cracked pepper, can be added for a touch of spice.

Peking Duck Sauce
Tien dou jiang

MAKES ABOUT ½ CUP

3½ fluid ounces hoisin sauce
2 tablespoons superfine (bar)
   sugar
2 tablespoons sesame oil
warm water, to combine
   ingredients

Combine all the ingredients with 2½ tablespoons warm water in a microwave-safe bowl and microwave on high for 30 seconds. Stir, and microwave an additional 30 seconds, until warm enough to dissolve the superfine sugar.

This sauce can be stored in the refrigerator for up to 2 weeks.

Garlic Dipping Sauce
Suan ni wei jiang

MAKES 2 TABLESPOONS

2 cloves garlic, finely chopped
1 teaspoon rice vinegar
2 teaspoons dark soy sauce
3 teaspoons light soy sauce
1 tablespoon superfine (bar)
   sugar
3 teaspoons sesame oil

In a small bowl, combine all the ingredients. Set aside for 10–20 minutes before use.

This sauce can be stored in the refrigerator for 3–4 days.

Steamed White Rice

SERVES 4–6

1¾ cups medium-grain white
  rice
water, to cook rice

Pour rice into a heavy-based saucepan with a tight-fitting lid. Add 2¾ cups water, cover with the lid, and bring to a boil over high heat. Reduce heat to very low and simmer the rice for 8–10 minutes, without lifting the lid. Remove pan from the heat and set aside, still covered, for 5 minutes before serving.

Sichuan Pepper–Salt
Hua jiao yun

MAKES ABOUT ⅓ CUP

1½ tablespoons Sichuan
  peppercorns
1¾ ounces fine table salt

Heat a wok or small fry pan, without oil, over medium heat. Toast the peppercorns for about 2 minutes, shaking the pan so they brown evenly. Remove peppercorns from the pan and grind to a fine powder in a spice grinder or mortar, then shake through a fine sieve.

Pour the salt into the wok or fry pan and heat gently for about 40 seconds, stirring slowly. Add the ground pepper and mix well, then place onto a plate to cool.

When completely cool, transfer mixture to a small spice jar. Pepper–salt will keep, stored in a cool dark place, for many months.

Chicken Stock

2 pounds 3 ounces fresh
   chicken necks or bones
¾-inch piece fresh ginger, cut
   in half
4 spring onions (white parts
   only)
3–4 Sichuan peppercorns or
   1 star anise (optional)
water, to prepare chicken stock

Place chicken necks or bones, ginger, spring onions and spices (if using) in a large saucepan and add 2¼ quarts water. Bring slowly to a boil, skimming the surface from time to time to remove surface foam and impurities.

Reduce heat to low and simmer very gently for about 1 hour (the liquid should barely bubble). Strain and discard the solids.

Chicken stock can be stored in the refrigerator for 2–3 days, or frozen for 2–3 months.

✳ For a richer stock, blanch a raw pork shank in boiling water and drain, then cook it with the chicken bones and seasonings for about 1½ hours.

Fish Stock

MAKES ABOUT 5 CUPS

2 pounds 3 ounces fish bones
  and heads
$1/3$ teaspoon fennel seeds,
  lightly crushed
1 small onion, cut in half
water, to prepare fish stock

Place the fish bones and heads in a pot with the fennel seeds and onion. Add 5 cups water and bring slowly to a boil. Skim surface, then decrease heat and simmer gently for about 15 minutes (the liquid should barely bubble). Strain and discard the solids.

Fish stock can be refrigerated for 2–3 days, or frozen for 2–3 months.

✳ Instead of fennel seeds, you could use a few stems from a fennel bulb, or a stick of celery.

✳ To make prawn-head stock, use heads and shells from 2 pounds 3 ounces prawns and omit the fennel seeds. After simmering, carefully pour into a conical strainer set over a bowl and crush the shells and heads with the end of a rolling pin to squeeze out as much liquid and color as possible. Use the stock at once, or freeze for up to 1 month.

Special Ingredients

BAMBOO SHOOTS These add a distinct earthy taste and delicious crunch to Chinese stir-fries, soups and braised dishes. Available as small cans of sliced bamboo shoots or larger cans of whole shoots or chunks. Ready-to-use fresh bamboo shoots are sold in some Asian stores.

BEAN PASTES OR SOY-BEAN PASTES These salty seasonings, not unlike miso, are made by grinding salt-fermented soy beans or broad beans. Garlic and/or chili powder are added to make potent sauces used mainly in Sichuan cooking. **Chili bean paste** (dou ban jiang la) and **garlic chili bean paste** keep for a long time in the refrigerator, and are sold in most Asian stores. These red, salty and intensely hot sauces give rich, deep flavor to stir-fries and braised dishes. Red miso together with chili powder can be substituted.

BLACK-SESAME PASTE A sweet dessert ingredient made by grinding black sesame seeds with sugar. Chestnut or lotus-seed paste, or sweet red-bean paste, can substitute, as could roasted and ground white sesame seeds sweetened with sugar.

CHESTNUT PASTE A sweet thick paste made from roasted chestnuts. It is sold in cans, ready to use, at well-stocked delicatessens and some Chinese food stores.

CHILI OIL (hong you) A mild seed oil infused with hot dried chili peppers. It is used in spicy stir-fries, sauces and dips. Make your own by steeping chili flakes in hot oil.

CHINESE FIVE-SPICE POWDER (wu xiang fen) An aromatic seasoning consisting of ground star anise, Sichuan pepper, cassia bark, fennel, and cloves or dried licorice root.

CHINESE GREENS A range of Chinese cabbages and other greens are sold in supermarkets and Chinese stores. Choy sum and gai larn have flat leaves, thick green stems and small flower heads, and may be known as Chinese broccoli. Broccoli and broccolini can replace them in any dish. Bok choy has fleshy white stems and soft leaves, while mustard greens (gai choy) are small and compact and have a slight bitterness. Chinese cabbage (wombok) has a firmly packed head with leaves that have a creamy-yellow thick base and pale-green crinkly tops.

CHINESE ROAST DUCK Peking-style roast duck, with its crisp, glossy amber skin, can be purchased ready-to-eat. If you do not have access to a specialty Chinese shop that roasts duck, check whether your butcher or delicatessen stocks packaged duck.

CHINESE SAUSAGE (lap cheong) A hard, dry, salami-like sausage made from pork, fat and spices. It adds an intriguing spiciness and chewy texture to rice dishes, stir-fries and stuffings. It will keep for months in the refrigerator. Available from Chinese food stores and some supermarkets.

COOKED OIL see oil

DUCK Use fresh duck for best flavor and tenderness. If using frozen duck, allow at least 10 hours for it to thaw in the refrigerator. See also Chinese roast duck.

DUMPLING WRAPPERS These can be purchased fresh or frozen from Asian food stores and some supermarkets. Work with them quickly to prevent drying out.

FIVE-SPICE SALT To make this salt, heat 2 tablespoons fine table salt in a wok for 1 minute. Remove wok from the heat and add 2 teaspoons Chinese five-spice powder. Cool.

GARLIC CHIVES These flat green leaves have a distinct garlic taste. They may be used in stir-fries and soups, and fillings for dumplings.

HOISIN SAUCE A thick, sweet sauce used in braised dishes and also as a dipping sauce. It can be found in Asian food stores and most supermarkets.

MANDARIN PEEL (chen pi) This fragrant dried citrus peel is used in braised and poached dishes, soups and some stir-fries for its distinct, fresh flavor. It's available at Chinese stores, or you can dry your own in a low oven, dehydrator or in the sun, and store in a glass jar. Tangerine peel can substitute.

NOODLES Fresh and dried Chinese **egg noodles** are made from a basic egg and flour dough, and are yellow in color. **Rice noodles** are also available fresh or dried. **Rice sheets** are uncut sheets of fresh rice-noodle dough. They can be used to make snack rolls or cut into ribbon noodles. **Dried rice vermicelli** can be quickly deep-fried to make a crunchy garnish or base for stir-fries. **Thick wheat-flour noodles** in the Shanghai tradition can be replaced by fresh Japanese udon noodles.

OILS (cai you) In general a mild seed oil (rape, canola or sunflower), nut oil (macadamina) or vegetable oil (corn or peanut) is used for cooking. **Sesame oil** (xiang you) can be used in conjunction with other cooking oils to add flavor, but it is not suitable as a primary frying oil. Flavorless light olive oil may be used, but the preferred oil in most Chinese stir-fries is **cooked oil**, which is oil that has previously been used for deep-frying – this is not only economical, but adds extra flavor to a dish and helps with browning. (Note that oil that has been used to deep-fry seafood should preferably be reused only once, for cooking other seafood, due to the strong flavors it retains.) Rendered pork fat (lard), chicken and duck fat are also sometimes used.

OYSTER MUSHROOMS These mild-flavored mushrooms have delicate caps on an off-center stem. Readily available from fresh food markets and supermarkets, they can be used in place of straw mushrooms or shiitakes.

PICKLED GINGER Also known as sushi ginger, this is ginger that has been sliced and pickled in brine or vinegar, which turns it a pale pink color. It can be rinsed and used in place of fresh ginger.

RED-BEAN PASTE Made from cooked and mashed adzuki beans (red beans), this canned product is used in sweet and savory soups, and fillings for buns and pastries. It is available sweetened or unsweetened and is sold at Chinese food stores.

RICE Medium-grain white rice is considered the best variety to accompany Chinese dishes, as the grains stick together making it easier to eat with chopsticks. Rice is cooked by the absorption method (see page 239). Allow about ⅓ cup uncooked rice per person. **Glutinous or 'sticky' rice** is sometimes eaten with Chinese meals, but is more usually used in sweet and savory snacks, clay pot dishes and desserts.

RICE WINE (liao jiu) Made from fermented rice, this clear or amber-colored wine has a mild, sake-like taste. Rice wine for cooking is often not suitable for drinking. It is available from supermarkets.

SALTED BLACK BEANS (dou chi) These dried, fermented and salted soy beans are wrinkly, dark and oily in appearance. They last for many months stored in a spice jar, and may be used whole or chopped in sauces. Bottled black-bean sauce can replace them in most recipes, with adjustments to the amount of salt and soy sauce added.

SALT-PICKLED VEGETABLES Pickled vegetables such as cabbage, radish, turnips and mustard greens (gai choy) are used in Chinese cooking for their pungent, salty taste. They are sold in jars and vacuum packs in Asian stores and some supermarkets. It is best to rinse off excess salt before use.

SESAME OIL see oil

SHIITAKE (BLACK) MUSHROOMS (xiang gu) These mushrooms have an intense aroma and pleasing spongy texture. Dried shiitakes must be soaked for 20–30 minutes in hot water before use, and the tough, woody stems trimmed off.

SHRIMP PASTE This paste gives a distinctive of-the-sea taste to dishes. For Chinese cooking choose the soft grey–pink variety for its milder flavor.

SICHUAN PEPPER (hua jiao) A spice native to China, the small red-brown berries are not related to pepper but have a similar peppery taste. Sichuan pepper has a numbing effect on the mouth and throat, so must be used with caution. Whole peppercorns are used in braised and poached dishes, and where ground pepper is called for, the seeds are toasted before grinding.

SOY SAUCE (jiang you) **Light soy sauce** is a salty seasoning used in cooking to make sauces and dressings, and as a condiment at the table. **Dark soy sauce**, which is sometimes labeled as mushroom soy, is less salty, darker and slightly thicker. It is used when a deep-brown glossy sauce, marinade or cooking liquid is needed. Look for a naturally fermented product for best flavor.

SPRING-ROLL WRAPPERS These dry, thin squares of flexible rice dough are not to be confused with the hard dry wrappers used for making Vietnamese rice-paper rolls.

STRAW MUSHROOMS These smooth-skinned, pale grey–pink mushrooms are occasionally available fresh, but are most commonly purchased canned. Unused mushrooms can be kept in lightly salted water for 3–4 days in the refrigerator.

SWEET RED-BEAN PASTE see red-bean paste

TOFU (doufu) Also known as bean curd, tofu is made from coagulated soy milk. Soft or silken tofu is extremely delicate and is used in soups and dishes where it can be cooked quickly and gently. To slice or dice soft tofu, hold it in the palm of your hand and carefully cut with a kitchen knife, then gently transfer from your hand to the dish. Firm tofu and fried tofu are used in stir-fries and braised dishes. Once opened, tofu is best used within a few days and cannot be frozen.

TOFU SKINS These flat sheets are made from the skin that forms on the surface when boiling soy milk to make tofu. They can be used as a crunchy wrapper for fried snacks and spring rolls.

VINEGAR (cu) Good-quality **Chinese black vinegar** has a mellow flavor similar to balsamic vinegar, although it is sweeter and less intense. **Chinese red vinegar** is fragrant and sweet but slightly tart. **White rice vinegar** is readily available at supermarkets and Asian stores, but can be replaced with cider vinegar in any recipe.

WATER SPINACH (tong cai) This Asian green has hollow stems and long pointed leaves. English spinach can replace it in any recipe.

WONTON WRAPPERS These small, thin squares of flour and egg dough are used for wrapping wontons and other dumplings. They are readily available from the refrigerator or freezer section of supermarkets. To make your own, prepare a standard pasta dough and roll it out on the finest setting of a pasta machine, then cut out 3½-inch rounds or squares. If dusted with cornstarch, homemade wonton wrappers can be frozen.

WOOD EAR FUNGUS Also known as black cloud ear fungus, wood ear has little taste but an intriguing crunchy texture. It is available fresh or dried. Dried wood ear fungus should be soaked in hot water for about 20 minutes before use (they will double or even triple in size) and any woody parts trimmed.

INDEX

PENGUIN BOOKS

Published by the Penguin Group
Penguin Group (USA) Inc., 375 Hudson Street, New York, NY 10014, U.S.A
Penguin Group (Canada), 90 Eglinton Avenue East, Suite 700, Toronto, Ontario, Canada M4P 2Y3 (a division of Pearson Penguin Canada Inc.)
Penguin Books Ltd, 80 Strand, London WC2R 0RL, England
Penguin Ireland, 25 St Stephen's Green, Dublin 2, Ireland (a division of Penguin Book Ltd)
Penguin Group (Australia), 250 Camberwell Road, Camberwell, Victoria 3124, Australia (a division of Pearson Australia Group PTY Ltd)
Penguin Books India Pvt Ltd, 11 Community Centre, Panchsheel Park, New Delhi – 110 017, India
Penguin Group (NZ), 67 Apollo Drive, Rosedale, North Shore 0632,
New Zealand (a division of Pearson New Zealand Ltd)
Penguin Books (South Africa) (Pty) Ltd, 24 Sturdee Avenue, Rosebank, Johannesburg 2196, South Africa

Penguin Books Ltd, Registered Offices: 80 Strand, London, WC2R 0RL, England

First published by Penguin Group (Australia), 2010
This edition published in 2012 by Penguin Group (USA) Inc.

ISBN: 978-0-14-320637-8

Special Markets ISBN: 978-0-14-219665-6

10 9 8 7 6 5 4 3 2 1

Designed by Marley Flory and Claire Tice © Penguin Group (Australia)
Photography by Julie Renouf
Food styling by Lee Blaylock
Typeset by Post Pre-press Group, Brisbane, Queensland
Scans and separations by Splitting Image, P/L, Clayton, Victoria

Printed in the United States of America